TIMPSON'S TOWNS
OF ENGLAND AND WALES

Oddities & Curiosities

JOHN TIMPSON

JARROLD

PICTURES *left to right*
- Monster turtle shell, Royal Victoria Hotel, Newport, Shropshire.
- Carved figures of musicians on Blagraves House, Barnard Castle, County Durham.
- Figure on pulpitum screen, Southwell Minster, Nottinghamshire.
- Monnow Bridge, Monmouth, Gwent.

TIMPSON'S TOWNS

Designed and produced by Parke Sutton Limited, Norwich
for Jarrold Publishing, Norwich

Text copyright © John Timpson 1989
This edition copyright © Jarrold Publishing 1989
First published 1989 by Jarrold Publishing
Paperback edition 1994
Reprinted 1995

ISBN 0-7117-0419-8 hardback   ISBN 0-7117-0682-4 paperback

Printed in Great Britain
Text typeface 10pt Berkeley Old Style Medium

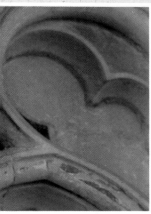

TIMPSON'S TOWNS
OF ENGLAND AND WALES

Oddities & Curiosities

JOHN TIMPSON

JARROLD

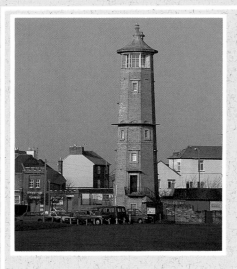

PICTURES *left to right*
- Lighthouse, Harwich, Essex.
- Effigy on the tomb of Penelope Boothby, Ashbourne parish church, Derbyshire.
- Medieval bridge, Wadebridge, Cornwall.
- Effigy above the door of the Blue House, Frome, Somerset.
- Brightly coloured barges on the canal at Birmingham, West Midlands.
- The Piece Hall, Halifax, West Yorkshire.

Contributors

AUTHOR
John Timpson O.B.E.

RESEARCHER
Jan Tavinor

DESIGNER
Geoff Staff

PHOTOGRAPHERS
Dennis Avon, John Brooks, Alan Guttridge, Neil Jinkerson, Charles Nicholas, Richard Tilbrook

ILLUSTRATOR
Libby Turner

CONTENTS

INTRODUCTION

I confess that I have never been over-fond of big towns. I subscribe to Cyril Connolly's view that no city should be too large to walk out of in a morning – except that I would reduce the limit to half an hour. And as the developers have moved in and character has been driven out, I have liked them even less. But our smaller country towns still retain the individual features of earlier, more eccentric generations, and even in the big cities, among the tower blocks and the shopping precincts and the industrial estates, one can still find the occasional reminder that there was life before concrete.

I found it difficult to define where big villages end and small towns begin. I used to live in a Hertfordshire commuter 'village' of over

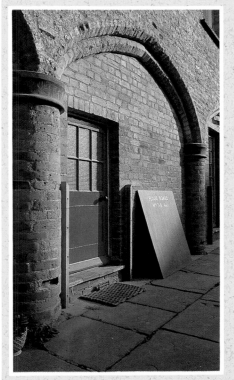

PICTURES *left to right*
- Hampton Court, King's Lynn, Norfolk.
- Heraldic crest, Sidney Sussex College, Cambridge, Cambridgeshire.
- Castellated tower, Beeston, Nottinghamshire.
- Earth maze, Saffron Walden, Essex.

7000 people, each one of whom was deeply offended when the council put up a direction sign to the 'Town Centre'. But in Norfolk, where I now live in a parish of forty-odd souls, a place that size would be a major conurbation. In the end I took the view that if St David's in Dyfed can be a cathedral city with a population of 2000, that was about the right size to qualify for this book.

I cannot of course mention them all. Some I am not sufficiently familiar with, others have already appeared in *Timpson's England*; and a few, alas, have been so thoroughly modernised, standardised and sanitised that the only remarkable thing about them is how anyone can bear to live there. Greater London I have omitted altogether; from every point of view, not just this book, it is far, far too big.

I am grateful to those readers of *Timpson's England* who told me about their own favourite sightings, and I hope they find their suggestions have been followed up. I am grateful also to those who pointed out the occasional error, and I hope they will forgive me if they find any in these pages. No matter how careful the checking, reference books are not all infallible and old tales can vary greatly in the telling.

It is quite possible too that some of my oddities and curiosities may have disappeared before you read about them, such is the rate of development in our towns and the destruction that goes with it. But at least they have been recorded and their memory preserved. I hope that all those I have mentioned will give you as much pleasure as they have given me.

JOHN TIMPSON O.B.E.

Should any readers wish to visit items mentioned in the book, pages 231 to 251 contain maps showing where they can be found. Each map is accompanied by an index giving a short description of each item, and where it is located.

A comprehensive subject index is included at the back of the book.

● Carved figure on the pulpitum screen, Southwell Minster, Southwell, Nottinghamshire.

● Southwell Minster, Southwell, Nottinghamshire.

WELCOME TO THE STREETS OF ADVENTURE

Sir Philip Gibbs christened Fleet Street 'The street of adventure', in the days when reporters stuck press passes in their hats, news editors shouted 'Hold the front page!' and nature correspondents were sent to cover wars in Ethiopia by mistake. Then the cynics altered it to 'The Street of Shame', most of the newspapers moved out anyway, and the only adventure left in Fleet Street is trying to cross it without being killed. But in towns all over England and Wales there are streets which really are an adventure, because even in the dullest row of buildings there can suddenly be one with a strange shape, or an eccentric façade, or a curious tale to tell. So step this way....

Sometimes a whole street can be an adventure in itself. We can step out of a modern shopping centre into surroundings which take us back a couple of centuries. For instance, most people have heard of the Lanes in Brighton in Sussex, that tangle of alleys where most of the shops are older than the antiques they sell. But just along the coast at **Worthing** there is another opportunity to take a step back in time. Although many of the 'ings' in the Worthing area are in danger of losing their identity in this expanding conurbation, Tarring manages to retain its original character while almost surrounded by modern development. The High Street still boasts two timber-framed houses from the fifteenth century, and there is the old village church, the village pub, and the village store. It likes to be known as a 'village within a town'; when Tarring says it isn't Worthing, it isn't joking.

The name of a street can hold as much history as the houses in it. One of my favourites is also in Sussex, Knockhundred Row in **Midhurst**. These days it might have been named in honour of Imran Khan or some other great Sussex batsman – all those Tun Streets could be in their honour too – but it actually dates back to medieval times, when the Lord of the Manor could form his own private army by summoning a hundred of his tenants to take up arms on his behalf. So a hundred front doors were knocked on, in streets like Knockhundred Row.

Just about every town has a High Street, but how many have two? **Brecon** in Powys found itself in this situation and

Tarring High Street, a village within a town. When Tarring says it isn't Worthing, it isn't joking.

named them High Street Superior and High Street Inferior. The inferior one seems to have died of shame, because it is difficult to find any trace of it in modern Brecon – the main streets have less common names, like the Bulwark and the Watton. High Street Superior, however, still survives and is still the way to the market. On market days it must feel very superior indeed.

With so many one-way systems in our towns there must be any number of 'double streets' – the traffic all going one way in one, and the other way in the other. But Double Street in **Framlingham**, Suffolk, got its name for quite a different reason. It was the first street in the town to have houses and shops on both sides

A Row to knock up a Hundred in Midhurst (above) and a Superior High Street in Brecon. Did the Inferior one die of shame?

HIGH ST SUPERIOR

of the road. Presumably this was such an unusual sight in rural Suffolk that people thought they were seeing double – and the name stuck.

A cobbled street is common enough in most old towns, but there are some very curious 'cobbles' you can walk on at **Wantage** in Oxfordshire. Dick Whittington was a frequent visitor to the town – it was the home of his wife's family, the Fitzwaryns – and if he was still looking for streets paved with gold he would have had quite a jolt in Wantage. They couldn't even run to proper cobble-stones for the passage which leads from Newbury Street to the almshouses; it is paved entirely with sheeps' knucklebones.

Before I move on to individual houses, there are some groups of them which flavour the character of the whole street. **Knutsford** in Cheshire is probably best

Streets with double trouble and cobble trouble. Double Street in Framlingham was the first to have a double row of shops and houses, and the name stuck; a passage in Wantage is cobbled, not with stones but knucklebones.

King's Coffee House in Knutsford, one of the eccentric creations of Richard Harding Watt.

known for being Mrs Gaskell's 'Cranford' and for having a service station named after it on the M6. But it was also the home of a splendid eccentric called Richard Harding Watt, who put up some very strange buildings indeed; so strange that one might think Knutsford got its name from him rather than King Cnut.

His individual creations are remarkable enough. King's Coffee House, for instance, is built in Italianate style with a lofty battlemented tower, and pillars which came from a derelict church in Manchester. One unkind critic wrote that he was grateful the High Street was so narrow, because it made it impossible to see more than a small section of the building at any one time.

Mr Watt also conjured up the Gaskell Memorial Tower and the Ruskin Rooms, which I can only describe as striking. But his biggest effort was a row of houses in Legh Road, where he lived himself, which the distinguished expert Sir Nikolaus Pevsner summed up crisply as 'the maddest sequence of villas in all England'.

Far more attractive, but with a rather unusual feature, is the terrace of Regency houses in Clifton, **Bristol**, known as the Paragon. The terrace forms an elegant crescent, but while the fronts of the houses are concave, the porches curve the other way, with convex double doors. The doors are all painted in different colours, which serves to emphasise this little idiosyncrasy. Perhaps the architect wanted to make it look different from Royal York Crescent, a nearby terrace of the same era.

More of Richard Harding Watt's Knutsford eccentricities – 'the maddest sequence of villas in all England' (above).

A more orthodox sequence, but unusual nonetheless, the Paragon in Bristol, where the house fronts are concave but the doors are convex (below).

Not a university college but homes for old people. The Gascoigne Almshouses in Aberford were perhaps a little too overwhelming for the old folk; they are now used as workshops.

Terraces of a very different style were built at the time of the Industrial Revolution in **Hebden Bridge**, the West Yorkshire mill town. The workers' cottages were packed in as tightly as possible. Elsewhere they would have been built back-to-back, but because they are on a steep hillside these are virtually bottom-to-top. Indeed from certain angles they look as if they were actually built on top of each other. A larger house was built at the end of each row for the foreman, like a corporal's quarters at the end of a barrack-room.

Almshouses offered another chance for architects to design a distinctive block of buildings. Those at **Aberford** in Yorkshire are a striking example. The Gascoigne Almshouses were built in 1844 to look more like a university college than old people's homes, with an imposing central tower as the focal point. It was all too much for the old people; they moved out and the City of Leeds moved in, to convert them into conservation workshops for the city's art gallery.

You will no doubt be familiar with **Conwy**'s claimant for Britain's smallest house, only 6 feet wide and 10 feet deep, though more remarkable than the house itself is how it accommodated its last tenant in 1900, a man of six foot three. Nor need I linger over the oldest inhabited house, Aaron's House in **Lincoln**, except to note that Aaron was a money-lender whose clients included King John, so the house could well have had 'By Appointment' over the door.

I am more taken with the eccentricities of the Egyptian House in **Penzance**, with its eagle and its coat of arms, its pillars and carved Egyptian servants, a place no self-respecting Pharaoh would be seen dead in – and they have been seen dead in some quite remarkable places. I gather the house was a copy of an exhibition hall in London's Piccadilly, where such excesses would not be quite so noticeable. It is difficult to understand why anyone would plant something quite so incongruous in a quiet Cornish town, but the Landmark Trust seemed to like it and restored it to its original ostentatious glory, and the National Trust now entices customers through its pillared portals to buy headscarves and car badges in its shop.

It is the sort of façade that would not look out of place on a flashy 1930s cinema, whereas there is a real cinema in **Salisbury** which has been inserted with remarkable discretion inside a fifteenth-century house. The modest entrance has been fitted under the original upper floors, which retain their high narrow windows, oak beams and heraldic shields. What a pity they had to hang in front of them the large vertical sign bearing the legend 'ODEON' in bogus Olde English lettering . . .

Egyptian servants above the door, ornamental pillars, tomb-shaped windows – but would a Pharaoh be seen dead in it? The Egyptian House in Penzance (left) is now a National Trust shop. The National Trust might be pleased that this Salisbury cinema (below) has preserved the original fifteenth-century façade – but a pity about the Olde English 'ODEON' down the front.

The very old Old House and the not-much-younger New Inn in Salisbury (above). What was the Old House called when it was young, one wonders. And what did they call the House of Nodding Gables in Tewkesbury (right) before the gables nodded, or the Crooked House in Stow-on-the-Wold (below) before it was crooked?

Fortunately Salisbury is rich in other old buildings which have so far escaped this kind of indignity. Two stand side by side in New Street: the Old House and the New Inn. The Old House is indeed 700 years old, a tall building with walls of flintstone and slate. The New Inn is a mere 500 years old, very Tudor with its low timbered walls, and indeed looking more venerable than the Old House next door. The house is actually a restaurant now, and it does have some Olde English lettering here and there, but not right down the front wall.

One wonders in these cases what the Old House was called when it was new; or indeed when the New Inn will admit to being old. And what was the House of Nodding Gables in **Tewkesbury** called before one of the supporting timbers gave way and caused a gable to lean over sideways? Like the Salisbury cinema, incidentally, its fine old frontage now sports a modern appendage; a large golden key indicates that a building society occupies the ground floor.

There is also the Crooked House at **Stow-on-the-Wold** in the Cotswolds, which leans quite steeply because of subsidence. But perhaps the most dramatic example of crooked architecture is the King's School shop in **Canterbury**, which not only leans itself but has an amazingly cock-eyed doorway, quite out of kilter with the shop windows on either side.

The shop's history has almost as many twists as its architecture. In Jacobean times it was known as Sir John Boys' house, though its bears the date 1617 and Sir John is known to have died in 1612. Perhaps he had problems with the builders, and they never did get it right even after his death. It was then occupied by a weaver and known as The Dutch House, until Olde English came into fashion and it became Ye Olde Curiosity Shoppe and then, inevitably, Ye Olde Tea Shoppe. When King's School took it over they sensibly corrected the spelling, though the fancy lettering remains.

The crookedness is blamed on the fact that it was originally one of a pair of houses, and when the other half was demolished it leaned over in sympathy.

That cock-eyed doorway, however, seems to defy explanation.

It is not all that unusual for an old building to get out of true, and the Booth Hall at **Evesham** in Worcestershire has a bend or two in its fifteenth-century timbers. But it still stands four-square, with straight walls and ninety-degree corners;

so why is it known as The Round House? Similarly there is a house in **Exmouth** called 'À la Ronde' which is actually octagonal. Its main claim to fame are the shell-covered walls inside it; the Quaker poet John Scott used the same sort of decoration for his Grotto, which stands in Scott's Road in **Ware**, Hertfordshire.

Some more curious angles. How did the King's School shop in Canterbury (above, left) get that cock-eyed door? And why is the obviously rectangular Booth House in Evesham (above) called the Round House!

'À la Ronde' in Exmouth – round, with angles. But the occupants were more interested in seashells than geometry.

The Merchant's House at Tenby has preserved its circular chimney stack (right) but the original painted flowers on an inside wall (above) were once covered by 23 coats of whitewash.

The Judge's House in Gloucester is tucked away up a passage 3 feet wide – creating a problem for enemies, and photographers!

Exmouth Tourist Board is very proud of its nearly-round house and has retained its not-quite-accurate name. Perhaps they feel 'À la Ronde' sounds more enticing to tourists than 'À l'Octagon'.

On the subject of names that have stuck, there are a couple in **Rye**, Sussex, which have an interesting story behind them; a cut above the Dunromin and Chez Nous genre. In Mermaid Street there is a house called simply The House Opposite; it is immediately opposite the Mermaid Inn. They must have been asked so often if they lived near the Mermaid that the name became permanent. And round the corner in West Street is The Other House. The carpenter who lived there found that another family in the street had the same name as his, and they so often had to direct his customers to 'the other house' that he gave it that name to make it simpler for them.

Going back to 'À la Ronde', it was built on the same plan as the church of San Vitale at Ravenna, but a house does not need to have such exotic origins – nor shells on its walls – to have a noteworthy feature. The Merchant's House at **Tenby**, for instance, is a very traditional design, so much so that it has a circular chimneystack, which was once character-istic of that region of Wales but is now very rarely seen. Not all the Merchant's House has remained unchanged over the years; when it was restored they found that the original painted flowers on an inside wall had been concealed under *twenty-three* coats of whitewash.

One of **Gloucester**'s finest old houses is tucked away behind a garden shop, up a passage only 3 feet wide. Maverdine House, also called the Judge's House, was the headquarters of Cromwell's com-mander, Colonel Massey, during the siege of the city in the Civil War, and he may have found it convenient to have such a narrow approach route, in case the Royalists came after him. Certainly it has made life difficult for photographers ever since.

On the subject of narrowness, Nell Gwyn's house in **Windsor** gives the impression of being only the width of the front door, but there is plenty of room inside. The sign which hangs outside it suggests it has become an inn, but Nell's former home is now a rather superior shop – with not an orange in sight.

The Blue House in **Frome** market-place makes its purpose much clearer. Above the entrance of this unusual building, with its high roof and cupola, is a stone effigy of a rather charming old lady, a reminder that this was 'a sanctuary and home for elderly Frome Ladies'. As they like to pronounce Frome 'Froom', I wondered if the Blue House used to claim: 'There's always rome in our home at Frome, we care from the cradle to the tome.' This has been firmly denied.

A building which served a similar purpose, but without an old lady over the door to advertise it, is the Matron's College in **Salisbury**, which provided a home for eight widows or spinster daughters of deceased clergy. The story goes – and unlike the Frome slogan, I did not invent it – that Bishop Seth Ward had it built because a lady he was fond of had married a poor cleric instead of marrying him, and she had been left destitute when her husband died. It seems a devious and expensive way to provide one's lost love with a home, but no doubt the seven other ladies who were able to move in with her thought it a splendid idea.

Two sorts of homes for two sorts of ladies. The Blue House in Frome (above) was 'a sanctuary and home for the elderly', with an old lady in stone above the door to emphasise it. The plaque on Nell Gwyn's house in Windsor (left) makes its purpose even clearer: it was one of her royal 'perks'.

The Matron's College in Salisbury, said to be built by a bishop as a kindly gesture to his lost love.

Sustenance for the wayfarer – a piece of bread and a mug of beer at the St Cross Hospital in Winchester (above); lodging, entertainment and fourpence at a hostel in Rochester (below).

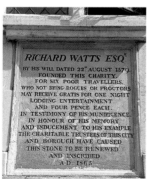

There are many other examples of slightly eccentric philanthropy which has resulted in some interesting buildings. At **Winchester**, for example, Bishop Henry of Blois founded the St Cross Hospital, a complex of almshouses, for the maintenance of thirteen poor men. That was the good news. The bad news was that they had to walk about in black gowns and medieval caps with the silver cross of St John on their left breasts, which was all right in 1136 but must make them feel a little conspicuous today.

Three hundred years after St Cross was founded, a supplementary set of almshouses was built by Cardinal Beaufort, and his chaps wear a mulberry-coloured gown with a tasselled cardinal's hat, which makes Bishop Henry's gear look pretty discreet by comparison. A needy traveller can still turn up at St Cross and receive the Wayfarer's Dole, a piece of bread and a mug of beer – and without having to put on a funny hat.

A wayfarer used to fare even better if he reported to the gabled building in **Rochester** High Street which bears the information over the door that

> *six poor travellers, who not being rogues or proctors, may receive gratis for one night their lodging, entertainment and 4d each.*

The hostel was founded in 1579 by a generous citizen called Sir Richard Watts. It was rebuilt in 1771 and the plaque was renewed in 1885, but the building is no longer open to wayfarers, and presumably the charity is administered in other ways. Charles Dickens, who included so much of Rochester in his novels, worked the hostel in also, though he thinly disguised it by writing of seven poor travellers instead of six.

Later do-gooders had other ways of doing good. In **Newark**, the Nottinghamshire town where King John died of over-eating, aided no doubt by a good quantity of ale to boot, the Victorians decided that such excesses should be discouraged, albeit a long time after the event. They built the Ossington Coffee Palace, a bizarre structure with timbered gables, a wooden balcony along one side and arches along another. It was dedicated to the joys of temperance, and presumably alcohol was not allowed on the premises. It is now a hotel and restaurant, and the proprietor would no doubt like me to stress that the ban no longer applies.

The Ossington Coffee Palace in Newark was dedicated to the joys of temperance. It has now changed its function, and presumably its attitude.

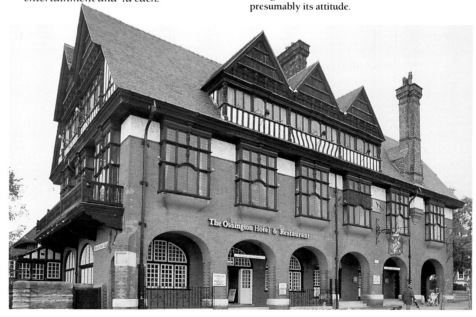

A lock cottage by the Leeds and Liverpool Canal at **Bingley** in West Yorkshire illustrates another Victorian virtue: thrift. Incorporated in the walls are letters cut in the bricks; they are in no particular order, some are on their sides, some are upside down. Can this be a coded message for passing barges? Actually it is an exercise in economy. The cottage was built with materials from a demolished warehouse in Liverpool, and the builders did not bother to keep the letters in their original order. If you have time to spare, you should be able to pick out all the letters in 'Leeds and Liverpool Canal Company'.

If that explanation seems a little unromantic, the tale attached to East Riddlesden Hall, a little way out of the town, amply makes up for it. This was the seventeenth-century home of the Murgatroyd family, whose reputation would have horrified the founders of the Ossington Coffee House. Their debauchery and profanity was so scandalous, it is said, that the River Aire changed its course to avoid their house. Fortunately the residents of the lock cottage have been far better behaved, or they might have had the same effect on the Leeds and Liverpool Canal.

As with East Riddlesden Hall, many houses are only remarkable because of the tales attached to them, like the Old Priest's House at **Prestbury** in Cheshire, which could be just another black-and-white medieval house (actually it is now just another black-and-white bank) except for the legend that goes with it. A priest who was refused access to his church during Cromwell's era risked his neck by preaching from the gallery which is still over the door.

Debauchery at East Riddlesden Hall (above), which changed the course of the river, and devotion at the Old Priest's House at Prestbury (below) in an effort to change the course of history.

Other buildings are remarkable for their changing roles over the years, and none more so, surely, than the Old Hall in **Gainsborough**, where Henry VIII was introduced to his sixth and last wife, Catherine Parr. Since its days as a royal dating agency it has been: a parish church, a linen factory, a corn exchange, a mechanics' institute, a church again (but this time United Reformed), a block of shops and tenements, a theatre, and after the Napoleonic wars, a soup-kitchen. A brief pause, then it became an inn, a sale-room, a ballroom, and finally a Masonic Temple.

Throughout this series of transformations – I make it twelve, counting the churches twice – it somehow retained the most complete medieval kitchen in the country, and its main hall has the finest single-arch braced roof. Let's hope the thirteenth change, if there is one, will not be unlucky for either.

Gainsborough Old Hall is one of those buildings where the main points of interest are inside, and I hesitate to mention those not open to the public, lest the occupiers find themselves besieged. For instance, the residents of the terraced houses beneath the East Cliff at **Dover** may not be keen for you to know that they have quite fascinating cellars, which have been cut into the cliff behind them. But elsewhere in Dover you would no doubt be welcome in the Roman Painted House, which has the oldest and best-preserved wall paintings, so it is claimed, north of the Alps.

The Old Hall at Gainsborough has undergone twelve different conversions, ranging from a linen factory to a Masonic Temple, but its medieval kitchen has survived them all.

Domestic delights in Dover: cellars cut into the white cliffs (above), ancient wall paintings in the Roman House (below).

There is a remarkable wall painting also in Conquest House, in **Canterbury**. This is now a shop, but it was once the inn which provided lodgings for the knights who murdered Thomas à Becket. The painting was not done by them – they were more interested in assassination than art – but by a painter who was working at the archbishop's palace, in quite a different era. He found he could not pay the bill for his lodgings, so instead of doing the washing-up he painted above the fireplace a copy of the archbishop's coat of arms, which he had been working on at the palace.

A more solemn mark was left behind in Smithill's Hall, **Bolton**, by the Protestant martyr George Marsh, who was taken there to be interrogated by a Catholic 'entrapper of heretics' and urged to recant. He refused to do so, and as he was led away to imprisonment and subsequent burning at the stake he stamped his foot on the stone floor and cried: 'Between me and them let God witness. If my cause be just, let this prayer of Thine unworthy servant be heard.' It did him little good in this world, but the impression of his footprint was miraculously preserved and can still be seen there – or something very like it. According to legend it becomes wet with fresh blood on each anniversary of his death.

An artistic reminder of an impecunious painter in Conquest House, Canterbury (left and below).

A grim reminder of a Protestant martyr in Smithill's Hall, Bolton.

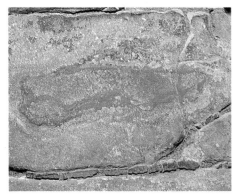

'God Damn Old Oliver' was the
message on this nail-studded
piece of wood in Welshpool
(right). Perhaps it was Cromwell
who knocked it about a bit.

A relic of a later religious upheaval
used to be on the outside wall of a house
in **Welshpool**, Powys, but the house is
now a restaurant and the relic has been
consigned to an ignominious site in a
passageway leading to the toilets. It is a
piece of wood studded with nails which
spell out, none too clearly, 'God Damn
Old Oliver'. We do not know if Cromwell
felt the effect.

The Isle of Man did not get too
involved in this sort of thing, but it does
have the odd concealed stairway and secret cellar, not built to conceal political
fugitives or persecuted priests but to faci-
litate a little smuggling. Bridge House in
Castletown has a good example of both;
the cellar for the contraband is below the
high water mark under the front lawn.
However, the Quayle family who lived
there were bankers as well as smugglers,

The double life of Bridge House
in Castletown, Isle of Man (right
and below). The Quayle family
ran a legitimate banking
business, and the concealed
stairway led to the strong-room,
but the cellar under the front
lawn had quite a different
purpose.

and the concealed stairway led to a per-fectly legitimate strongroom. The two sets of accounts they kept must have made fascinating reading.

Finally some strange homes which were not houses at all. Britain's cavemen did not all die out with the Ancient Britons; one can find cave houses in the streets of a number of towns in the Mid-lands and the North. Above the little town of **Kinver** in the West Midlands are the cave-dwellings of Holy Austin Rock, with holes in the hillside to act as chim-neys and a well outside the entrance. They are first mentioned in 1777, and there were still twelve families living in them in 1871 – the last one only moved out in the 1930s. At first glance they

Britain still had cavemen long after the Ancient Britons. The cave dwellings of Holy Austin Rock, above Kinver in the West Midlands, still had twelve families living in them in 1871, and the last resident only moved out in the 1930s. There are holes in the hillside to act as chimneys, and a well beside the entrance.

reminded me of the sandstone caves of Petra in Jordan, 'the rose-red city, half as old as Time'. But the brickwork which has been used to shore up some of the rock-face rather spoils the effect.

Mansfield in Nottinghamshire has similar cliff dwellings cut in the sandstone beside the Southwell road, where people were still living at the turn of the century. One or two have been given a proper chimney and a pantiled roof. But the real luxury model, the stately home of the cave-dwelling community, is at **Knaresborough** in Yorkshire. An eighteenth-century weaver called Thomas Hill spent sixteen years of his spare time creating a mansion for himself in the cliff. He called it Fort Montagu, gave himself a title and issued his own banknotes.

This rather overshadowed his cave-dwelling neighbour, a soothsayer called Mother Shipton who lived in a one-room establishment and slept on a rock bed. Nevertheless she achieved more lasting fame than the flamboyant Mr Hill, since some of her prophecies turned out to be right. She forecast that men would sail the seas in iron ships, fly through the air in machines and walk and talk under water. She also forecast that the world would end in 1861. You can't win them all . . .

To round off, literally, these streets of adventure, there is the 'dartboard round-about' at **Hemel Hempstead**, a motoring maze which I think has no equal anywhere else in Britain. It consists of half a dozen mini-roundabouts, adjoining each other in a large circle. At each mini-roundabout the usual rule applies about giving way to traffic from the right, but once you start weaving through them it is difficult to work out who has priority. In addition there are two lanes round each roundabout, so you have to plan three roundabouts in advance, which lane you need to be in to leave at the right exit . . .

I have known people take ten minutes or more to find their way round the 'dartboard'. Sometimes I have met the same chap two or three times making unplanned extra circuits. There can be long pauses at each roundabout while everyone waits for everyone else to make a move; and there are moments of drama when a despairing driver gives up the struggle and makes a beeline for his exit, straight across roundabouts, double lanes and unwary cyclists.

You shouldn't miss this fun-filled experience; but remember to take sandwiches.

Rather more luxurious cave dwellings were cut into the sandstone cliff at Mansfield. They were given elegant brick frontages, and one or two had real chimneys and pantiled roofs. The caves were just as un-cavelike inside.

Here we go round the multi-mini-roundabouts; a test of nerve at Hemel Hempstead.

I Was Walking In The Park One Day . . .

And I was taken by surprise, not by a pair of roving eyes, but by the oddities that have been planted in so many of them by whimsical benefactors or eccentric councils. A Gothic gateway here, a fussy fountain there, an appallingly ugly obelisk round the corner. Strange little buildings lurk behind the flowerbeds – and not all of them are public lavatories.

Sometimes the parks themselves have a chequered history. They may have been created, not as a generous gesture to the citizenry, but to conceal something nasty that had been there before. 'Parks', wrote George Gissing, 'are but pavement disguised with a growth of grass.' But they can be a lot more than that . . .

Public parks as we know them today – 'recreation grounds' provided by the local authority out of the rates – have only been around for a century or so, but even in pre-Christian times there were opportunities for the townsfolk to disport themselves on open spaces, where a leisure activity was provided for them in the form of a maze. These were not the baffling creations of laurel hedge and yew to be found at Hampton Court or Hatfield House, they were just patterns cut in the turf, so you could actually see which route to take before you started, and the end was always in sight.

Their purpose was not to puzzle, but to inspire. Many experts connect them with some early religious ritual, representing the twists and turns of the path through life. Others say they are part of a fertility rite, though the open-plan layout offers less opportunity for testing its effectiveness than the modern, more discreet equivalent.

The best surviving earth maze in Britain is claimed to be at **Saffron Walden**, where there was enough space left among the saffron crocus beds to cut a circular maze in the turf. It can still be explored on the common at the east end of the town.

Winchester has one too, but on a rather less convenient site, at the summit of St Catherine's Hill. It is known as a Miz

A pre-Christian religious ritual, or just a bit of fun for the kiddies before they invented swings? The circular earth maze at Saffron Walden.

Maze, and some say it is prehistoric, but a very similar Miz Maze at Breamore in Hampshire is said to be only medieval. No doubt both of them have been smartened up over the years, so it is difficult for even the experts to be certain.

By Elizabethan times towndwellers had more to enjoy in the way of outdoor sports on their open spaces, ranging from archery to executions. While countryfolk were losing their common land to unscrupulous gentry, much to the annoyance of Robert Kett and other rebellious rustics, their urban cousins did manage to hang on to stretches of greensward on which to frolic. The history of Chapelfield Gardens in **Norwich**, which has been a public park for over 400 years, is typical of many historic urban playgrounds.

Originally the gardens were the grounds around a college for priests. When that was closed down during the Reformation it was bought by the city fathers at a knock-down price, and came to be used for archery practice by the Tudor equivalent of the Territorial Army.

The clothworkers also used it for drying out their famous worsted cloth. And no doubt courting couples found a use for it too.

In Jacobean times Chapelfield Gardens and other such areas were the scene of much roistering, merrymaking and general hullabaloo. In Norwich a public warning was proclaimed 'not to spoil the grass by immoderate Campings and Dancing'. Camping was not the peaceful pursuit it is today; it was a particularly vicious form of mass football, with the object of kicking your opponents rather than the ball.

The days of the Regency brought more elegant pursuits to what became known as 'pleasure gardens', and in 1761 an enlightened Lord Mayor, Sir Thomas Churchman, laid out Chapelfield Gardens as a public park, with paths and flowerbeds and trees, in the style we are familiar with today. The date is interesting, because at least two other places claim to have had the first public park in Britain – and they only date from the 1840s.

Chapelfield Gardens in Norwich, a public park since Elizabethan Territorials used it for archery practice and clothworkers used it to dry out their worsted – preferably not at the same time.

Derby has its arboretum, presented to the town by the industrialist Joseph Strutt and opened as 'Britain's first public park' in 1840. For many years it boasted a statue of another notable manufacturer, Sir Henry Royce, but that has now been moved to the factory which still makes his cars.

Meanwhile **Birkenhead**, which had developed rapidly from a quiet Mersey-side village into a major shipbuilding town, acquired Birkenhead Park – 'the first purpose-built public park in the land'. It was created on what was described in 1842 as 'a low, foul-smelling swamp'. Five years later there were groves, gardens, fountains, two lakes, drives, 'and numerous sources of pleasure'. There are three entrance lodges in different styles – Gothic, Norman and Italian – and a massive main entrance, all arches and columns, copied from a temple in Athens. Creating parks in those days was as much a job for architects as landscape gardeners. Needless to say this all impressed the Americans enormously, and they imitated some of the park's features in New York's Central Park.

But which was really the first public park? Let's keep everyone happy, and say that Norwich has the first park laid out by a Lord Mayor, Derby the first park to contain a statue of Sir Henry Royce, and Birkenhead has the first park built on a low, foul-smelling swamp. None of them can really compete with Adam and Eve's . . .

A number of parks and gardens were created on the sites of old battles, or where battles might have been. The Gun

Sir Henry Royce (above) used to stand in Derby's arboretum, claimed to be Britain's first public park. But Birkenhead Park (right), with its massive main entrance, was not far behind. Certainly it was the first to be built created on 'a low, foul-smelling swamp'.

The Gun Garden at Rye was once a defence battery, to protect the town from the French. These days the gun is only for show. Ypres Tower was not named after a more recent battle; it was owned by John de Ypres in the fifteenth century – not for very long, but the name stuck.

Garden at **Rye** in Sussex, for instance, was the site of a defence battery, back in the days when Rye was a port and regularly thumped by the French. The tower alongside it is called Ypres Tower, a name which conjures up memories of more recent battlefields, but it was actually named after John de Ypres, who bought it in the fifteenth century when the town fathers needed a little ready money. They bought it back in the next century and used it as a prison, but the name stuck. The defence battery was converted into a bowling green, and now it is a terraced public garden with pleasant views over the river, where the sea – and the French – used to be.

The origin of Rye's Gun Garden is indicated by its name, and so is that of the Curfew Garden at **Midhurst** in Sussex.

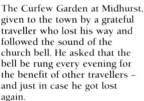

The Curfew Garden at Midhurst, given to the town by a grateful traveller who lost his way and followed the sound of the church bell. He asked that the bell be rung every evening for the benefit of other travellers – and just in case he got lost again.

According to local legend a traveller got lost in the neighbourhood one night and found his way to Midhurst by following the sound of the church bell. As a token of gratitude he bought the piece of land now called Curfew Garden and gave it to the town in return for the church bell being rung every evening – just in case he got lost again. The garden these days is attractively laid out with lawns and flower-beds, and the church bell is still rung at eight o'clock every night.

There is a much more macabre story, as you might expect from its name, behind a park in **Sheffield** known as the Cholera Gardens. More than four hundred people died in the epidemic which swept through the city in 1832, and most of them are buried in mass graves in these gardens. In the centre is a lofty, if rather spindly obelisk, like an ornate church steeple, in memory of the victims.

The Royal Victoria Park in **Bath** also has an obelisk, but with a much happier history. It was erected in 1837 to mark the coming of age of Princess Victoria. Having put it up, the good burghers of Bath decided to make further use of it to chronicle her reign. On its triangular base are depicted her marriage, the death of Prince Albert, and her illustrious position as Empress of India. They also provided three lions to guard it; one looks very superior, obviously proud of his assignment, another is profoundly thoughtful, perhaps wondering if he could be having more fun elsewhere, and the third is quite certain he could be, and is yawning widely . . .

The story of John Kay is also lavishly illustrated, but without any lions, on the monument in the gardens named after him at **Bury**, in Lancashire. Mr Kay invented the flying shuttle, a device which has no connection with the NASA

The obelisk in Cholera Gardens, Sheffield (left), where victims of an epidemic in 1832 were buried in mass graves. The obelisk in the Royal Victoria Park in Bath (above) has a happier history, commemorating the reign of Queen Victoria – but its guardian lions seem to find it rather boring.

Space Center but in its own way it also marked an historic advance in the speed with which man can operate. When he introduced the shuttle in 1738 it revolutionised the textile industry, and the chap who designed Kay's monument 170 years later, a Mr Gough of Bristol, was determined that nobody would forget it.

He created a domed pavilion with bronze panels showing textile machinery, and four statues depicting weaving, engineering, mining and agriculture – though weaving would have been enough to make the point. He rounded it all off with a portrait of John Kay on the front. Nobody could say that Mr Gough came to Bury, not to praise him ...

An assortment of park-aphernalia. A pinnacle from the House of Commons in the Rose Garden at Clitheroe (above), William IV sculptured by 'one of the rude sons of art' in Montpellier Gardens, Cheltenham (above, right), and an elaborate but out-of-action fountain in East Park, Southampton (right).

Cheltenham, famous for elegance and culture, with its colleges, its festivals, and its Gold Cup, rather surprisingly went for economy rather than class when it erected a statute of William IV in Montpellier Gardens. According to a town guide published in 1834, the statue was the work of 'one of the rude sons of art, a self-taught stonemason'. Nevertheless he made quite a good job of it; one can tell straight away from the crown that it is a king.

Southampton's parks are liberally sprinkled with monuments and statues. Gordon of Khartoum has an elaborate memorial in Queen's Park, though his link with the town is somewhat tenuous – he once happened to stay there with his sister. At the southern end of the common is one of the memorials to the crew of the *Titanic*, which sailed from Southampton on its fatal voyage. This one commemorates the stewards, sailors and firemen on board, while another in East Park is in memory of the engineer officers. Also in East Park, commemorating a former mayor of Southampton, is that favourite adornment of the public park, a fountain. In this case, a very large fountain, topped by a canopy held up by six pillars with a statue of Mr Andrews on top; and at the last visit, completely unusable.

Fountains bubble up in places other than parks, as indeed do statues, and I deal with some of the odder ones in other locations elsewhere. Less common is the ornament that has been put in the Rose Garden at **Clitheroe** in Lancashire, just below the castle. It stands in the middle of a flower-bed and seems to serve no purpose at all, unless it be to start an argument among passers-by about its identity. I doubt if they would ever guess. It is actually one of the pinnacles from the roof of the old Palace of Westminster, acquired for reasons and by methods unknown by Sir William Brass MP, later Baron Chattisham. Having acquired it Sir William probably had no idea what to do with it, so he gave it to Clitheroe Council in the 1930s. The Council couldn't have known what to do with it either, and possibly in desperation they dumped it in the Rose Garden, perhaps hoping it would soon be concealed by ramblers. But it still stands naked, and possibly a little ashamed, sticking out of its attractive surroundings like a sore stone thumb.

The ancient guilds of **Shrewsbury** had a much pleasanter way of ornamenting the Quarry Gardens, which lie between the river and the town walls. Each guild erected a rustic arbour, which foliage was able to cover much more readily than stone pinnacles. Alas, only one survives, the Shoemakers' Arbour, now behind a locked gate. The whole of the formal garden, known as the Dingle, is something of a memorial in itself; it was created by the late Percy Thrower, Britain's best known gardener since Capability Brown.

A rather different example of the horticulturist's art is the Bishop's Garden – more correctly Gardd yr Esgob – between the cathedral and the town hall at **Bangor** in Gwynedd. The town hall was in fact the bishop's residence. The bishopric is the oldest in Britain, older even than Canterbury, going back to the sixth century, and sometime between then and now a remarkable 'Biblical Garden' was created for the bishop, containing as many of the trees and plants and shrubs mentioned in the Bible as could adjust to the difference in climate between the West Bank and West Wales. I see the labels have not survived, but they were planted along 'Bible Walk' in the order in which they are mentioned in the Bible – so if you recognise one plant and you have a Bible handy, it shouldn't take more than a week or two to identify the rest.

A collection of plants based on botanical research, rather than Biblical reference, has been created in the **Oxford** University Botanic Garden, near Magdalen Bridge. What strikes the eye more forcefully than the plants themselves are the gateways into the Garden, seventeenth-century Doric archways with figures in the recesses, very grand and imposing for a garden gate.

Not bad for a garden gate – the impressive entrance to the Oxford University Botanic Garden (below).

The Shoemakers' Arbour in Quarry Gardens, Shrewsbury (far left), is the last of several provided by the town's guilds. The Bible Garden at Bangor (left) has Biblical plants and shrubs which have adjusted to the difference in climate between the West Bank and West Wales.

Over in **Cambridge**, not to be outdone, there is a mulberry tree in the Fellows' Garden at Christ's College with a curious historical significance. It is supposed to have been planted by the poet and author John Milton, at the behest of James I, who was keen to encourage the silk industry. Silkworms feed on the leaves of mulberry trees, and the idea was to increase the English silkworm population. It seems unlikely that many Fellows of Christ's College went into silk production, but they can still enjoy the sight of 'Milton's mulberry tree'.

I have put the quotation marks because the Fellow who currently holds the delightful title of Honorary Garden

Milton's mulberry tree in the Fellows' Garden at Christ's College, Cambridge (above), for the entertainment of silkworms, and the oak tree on Broadwater Green, Worthing (right), for the entertainment of skeletons.

The oldest resident of Sheffield's Botanical Gardens, a fossilised tree-stump estimated to be 250 million years old – but it's no good just counting the rings . . .

Steward, Dr David Coombe, has researched the tree's history down to the last mulberry, and can find no mention of it earlier than 1795. Since Milton was at the university in 1632 this raises understandable doubts in Dr Coombe's mind. He writes scathingly of an earlier chronicler who devoted four pages of text to linking Milton with the tree – 'full of wild speculation, mawkish prose, and an atrocious sonnet'. At least I have only occupied a couple of paragraphs – and not attempted a sonnet . . .

Another tree with a tale, though in less illustrious surroundings, stands at the end of Broadwater Green in **Worthing**. This highly respectable retirement haven is not immediately associated with tales of the macabre, but it is said that on Midsummer Eve a group of skeletons appears (is the collective noun 'a rattle'?) and they dance hand in hand – or bones in bones –

around this oak tree until the first cock crows. The tree is now isolated on a small triangle of land in the middle of a busy road intersection, so the spectral dancers may have difficulty in reaching their rendezvous. Perhaps some sort of lollipop lady could assist them, equipped with a skeleton staff.

As for trees which have long since expired, I suppose **Sheffield** can claim the oldest remains of a town tree in Britain. It was once in High Hazels Park but is now kept in more secure surroundings in the Botanical Gardens, a fossilised stump which is estimated to be 250 million years old. I emphasise oldest *town* tree, because a village in County Durham has a tree stump which is believed to be much the same age, give or take a million years. But that one looks like a large stone carbuncle; Sheffield's does at least look like the bole and roots of a tree.

Fascinating flooring: John Kyrle's summer-house in Ross-on-Wye has a mosaic swan made of horses' teeth (above) and the friars' house over the stream in the Franciscan Gardens in Canterbury has a trapdoor for fishing (right).

From Nature's eccentricities to manmade curiosities. John Kyrle of **Ross-on-Wye**, known as 'The Man of Ross' because of his great generosity to the town, provided its first water supply, repaired the church spire and donated a walled garden for public enjoyment. But it is his own back garden, now open to visitors on request, which contains his most unusual legacy. It has a summer-house with a mosaic floor depicting a swan. Nothing unusual about a swan, except that this one is made entirely of horses' teeth. Was Mr Kyrle, one wonders, a collector of equine molars, or did he have some understanding with the local knacker's yard? And why a swan, not a horse? Fascinating stuff . . .

A very different kind of building with an unusual feature in its floor still stands in the Franciscan Gardens in **Canterbury**. The Gardens once belonged to the Grey Friars, who made this their first head-quarters in England in the thirteenth century. They built a church and living quarters on the site, but only one house remains, built on arches over the river, and in its back room there is a trapdoor in the floor opening on to the water below. One could be forgiven for assuming this was an early Franciscan loo, but actually it was used for drawing up water, and there is still a bucket available for the purpose.

In the gardens behind the Royal Shakespeare Theatre at **Stratford-upon-Avon**, instead of a tennis court or a croquet lawn, there is a kind of chess-board cut into the turf. It is used in a very Shakespearian sport, Nine Men's Morris, as popular in his day among the good folk of Stratford as bowls is today. It is an open air version of chess, draughts and Chinese chequers rolled into one.

Boating ponds are common enough in parks, but few can equal the vast artificial pond in the Marine Hall gardens at **Fleet-wood** in Lancashire. It looks more like an Olympic swimming pool than a pond, but it is actually claimed to be the biggest

Unusual recreation facilities in public parks: the theatre gardens at Stratford-upon-Avon are marked out for Nine Men's Morris (above); the Marine Hall Gardens at Fleetwood have the biggest model yacht lake in Europe – it looks more like an Olympic pool.

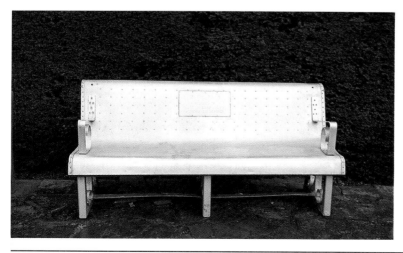

The Doctor's Pond linked with a lifeboat at Great Dunmow (above) and the park bench linked with a bomber in the Abbey Gardens at Bury St Edmunds.

model yacht lake in Europe. On windy days the water gets quite choppy, and it would seem to be the ideal place for testing out, say, the first model lifeboat, but that was actually done on the far more serene waters of the pond at **Great Dunmow** in Essex. It is known as the Doctor's Pond because Dr Lionel Lukin carried out the first lifeboat experiments on it in 1785. It seems a strange place to choose, so far from the sea; how for instance did he simulate a force-nine gale on those peaceful waters? But his experiment obviously worked; how often does a lifeboat sink?

Finally another uncommon story behind another common feature in parks – the park bench. At **Bury St Edmunds** in Suffolk there is a bench in the Abbey Gardens which commemorates American soldiers and airmen stationed in the area during the Second World War. It does not have just a plaque on it, as commemorative benches usually do. This one was constructed from the metal framework of an American 'Flying Fortress', one of the most famous bombers of the war. It is fitting that a relic of a twentieth-century conflict in the cause of freedom should be placed in the ruins of an abbey where, 700 years earlier, King John's barons got together in the cause of freedom and agreed on the Magna Carta.

LIFT UP YOUR EYES UNTO THE WALLS

The higher you lift them in most towns, the more interesting things there are to see. The first floor above a modern shop front may still have its oak beams and its latticed windows; the roof above that may still have its steep gables and its decorated chimneys. But what I have in mind are not general impressions but particular objects, put there to embellish, to impress, or just to amuse. Let us not now praise famous men – I shall not list all those commemorative plaques. Instead let us praise those often unknown men who devised something a little different – and stuck it on the wall.

I know of no city centre where the walls of the houses and shops are more richly decorated than **York**. A few steps away from the familiar glories of York Minster, in the maze of old city streets, there are all manner of unexpected delights. One of my favourites is the Red Indian in feathered head-dress and skirt, perched above a shoe shop in Petergate. Another is the horned red devil which glares down malevolently from a wall in Stonegate, fortunately restrained by a chain around his waist. Now that Stonegate has been pedestrianised it is safe to stand and stare back.

The most elegant of these figures is the little admiral who stands above the clock outside St Martin's in Coney Street, in immaculate blue and gold tailcoat and tri-corne hat, white waistcoat, breeches and

Some of the delightful wall decorations in the older streets of York – a frilly-skirted Red Indian, a horned red devil, and the little admiral perched on a clock in Coney Street.

Ye Olde Naked Man Cafe at Settle with ye olde naked man in the wall, protecting his modesty with a carpenter's plane (above). If indeed he was a carpenter as well as a naturist, one hopes he handled his tools with care. Rather more care perhaps than the artist who is said to have been responsible for creating the Liver Bird (left). He was supposed to include an eagle in Liverpool's coat of arms, but he was not too good at drawing eagles and this is how his efforts ended up. Rather than spend more money on another artist the city fathers made the best of a bad job – and the Liver Bird was born. Or so it is said . . .

stockings, carefully taking a sighting to ensure that York is sailing on the right course.

Rather less elegant, without tailcoat, waistcoat or even breeches, is the figure who looks across the Market Place at **Settle** in North Yorkshire, from the front of the Naked Man Cafe. It is indeed a naked man, set into the wall when it was built in 1663; but he is discreetly protecting his modesty with a skilfully placed carpenter's plane. A chair and a coffin are also depicted, indicating that he was a carpenter as well as a naturist. One hopes he handled his tools with care.

Animals and birds, real and imaginary, squat or perch in wood or stone all over the buildings of our towns and cities, and none is more famous or more prominent than the Liver Birds which top the Liver Buildings in **Liverpool**. They are much better known than Felix Rossi's far more valuable figure of Minerva, which shares the waterfront skyline with them from the roof of the town hall.

The popular story is that these rather unlovely birds frequented the pool which the village of Liverpool stood beside, and in due course were incorporated, for old times' sake, in the city's coat of arms. I have heard, however, that it didn't happen quite like that. The artist who designed the coat of arms was actually instructed to include an eagle, the

Varsity Varieties. An Oxford hyena with owl and man's head . . .

emblem of the city's patron, St John the Evangelist. Unfortunately he was not too good at eagles. His version came out a little oddly, but the city fathers decided to make the best of it – and the Liver Bird was born. Had they sacked him and employed an artist who was better at birds, would their descendants now be living in Eaglepool?

Some of the ancient colleges of **Oxford** have positive flocks of mythical creatures on their walls. Amid such a wealth of magnificent architecture it is perhaps impertinent just to pick out the oddities, but oddities there are in great abundance. Magdalen College, for instance, is a splendid place for lifting up the eyes, and not just to watch the choristers singing on top of the tower on May Day morning. Along the walls of the cloisters is an astonishing assortment of carved figures, some human, some animal, some a bit of each, representing all manner of virtues and vices.

Some are clearly Biblical – Goliath flexing his muscles, David slaying the lion, Moses taking the tablets. We also have Jacob holding hands with the Angel, looking rather like contestants in 'Come Dancing'. Then there is a schoolmaster, a physician, and a bearded character representing anger, with clenched fists raised above his head in the style of wrestler Big Daddy.

Among the birds and animals are a dejected eagle, a lion which its paw raised in salute, and a seated hippopotamus with a baby hippo on its back – not too easy to recognise, as the artist seemed to know as much about hippos as his Liverpool colleague knew about eagles . . .

Perhaps the most curious in the collection is the hyena holding an owl in one paw and a man's head in the other. An ancient guidebook says this represents fraud, and leaves it to the reader to work out why. A more recent writer homes in on the owl and says it symbolises learning; the owl's wisdom is presumably being transmitted by the hyena into the man's head. My own theory is that the mason was left with a spare owl and an extra head, and couldn't think where else to put them.

I must not leave **Cambridge** out of this. There are some odd specimens there too, as anyone who went to Oxford will confirm. I rather fancy the two strange animals which are holding up the coat of arms of the Beaufort family on the gateway of St John's College. Their name is shared with another university, with which they have absolutely no connection. They are called yales, mythical beasts with the bodies of antelopes and the heads of goats – and horns which

. . . and Cambridge yales, with the bodies of antelopes, the heads of goats, and horns which can swivel like gun turrets.

they can swivel. Unfortunately these are not working models, but they look striking enough none the less.

A working model does appear on the wall of another Cambridge college. The dial in the Old Court of Queen's College is one of the few sundials which can tell the time in the dark; it is a moondial too. It has the standard arrangement of a shadow being cast on the dial by the sun, but there is also a table of figures from which you can calculate the time at night by the shadow cast by the moon. It gives the date, the times of sunrise and sunset, the appropriate sign of the Zodiac and the altitude of the sun – though you may need a Cambridge degree in sundial-reading to work it all out.

At Queen's College, Cambridge, one of the few sundials which can still tell the time at night – so long as there is a moon. It offers other data too, but you may need a degree in sundial-reading to work it out.

Sparrow-hawks peer down from rainpipes and weather-vanes at Towneley Hall, Burnley; they were the family crest of the Towneleys (above). The Stanleys, however, favoured the porcupine, and a bright blue one lurks incongruously among the ancient timbers of Lord Leycester's Hospital in Warwick (below).

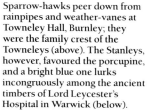

Returning to less intellectual wall decorations, creatures often appeared on a building because they were part of the family coat of arms or had some special significance for the occupants. Sparrow-hawks, for instance, fly all over the rain pipes at Towneley Hall in **Burnley**, and one is perched on the weather-vane. The bird was the family crest of the Towne-leys, and although their magnificent home has long been handed over to the the town, and the majestic circular drive is now lined with garden seats, the Towneley sparrow-hawks fly on.

Lord Leycester's Hospital is probably the most famous medieval building in **Warwick**, once the Guild House of St George, then almshouses, then a hospice. Disconcertingly, in the midst of all the oak beams and gables, there lurks a bright blue porcupine with a collar and chain and most ferocious-looking quills. It is not there to impale the pigeons, it is the crest of the Stanley family, who were linked with the Leycesters.

There is a different kind of explanation for the salamander which crawls up the wall of Churche's Mansion in **Nantwich**,

Cheshire. Much of the town was destroyed by fire in 1583, and the mansion was one of only three large buildings to survive. It was the home of Richard Churche, a wealthy salt merchant; when he built it 6 years earlier he had the foresight to put a salamander on it – according to legend the creature cannot be destroyed by fire. This early form of fire protection was obviously effective, and although the restaurant which now occupies the ground floor probably has a more sophisticated insurance policy, the salamander is still on duty.

Incidentally the great fire of Nantwich is recalled by a decoration on another house in the town; it is a verse carved on the home of Thomas Cleese in the Square. The first Queen Elizabeth organised a national appeal to rebuild the town and donated to it generously herself. A grateful Mr Cleese wrote the verse in her honour:

God grant our Royal Queen,
In England longe to Raign,
For she hath put her helping Hand
to bild this town againe.

And he renamed his home, Queen's Aid House.

Another town which suffered heavily from fires in the seventeenth century – it had three altogether – was **Marlborough** in Wiltshire. The first destroyed over 250 buildings and was declared a national disaster. Nevertheless the citizens continued to be careless with their matches and there were two more outbreaks in the next 40 years. It reached the stage where Parliament passed an Act forbidding the use of thatch in the centre of the town. Most of Marlborough had to be rebuilt, but some of the old medieval houses still survive, and in the Silverless Street area some still have their original wooden shutters, which escaped all three fires.

Some wall decorations which have survived the centuries were put there, it seems, just for the fun of it. William Beaumont, the first Mayor of **Warrington**, cheered up the red-brick frontage of his eighteenth-century house by adding stone panels depicting almost anything from a winged horse to a boy on a

An early form of fire insurance – the salamander (right), which according to legend is impervious to fire, successfully protected Churche's Mansion in Nantwich when much of the town was destroyed (above). Much of Marlborough was burnt down too, but the original wooden shutters on these cottages survived (below).

Fun and games on the wall. A house frontage in Ashburton (right) featured card suits; a mock Tudor block in Beverley (below) is decorated with Punch cartoons.

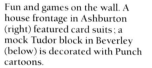

The Siege House in Colchester still has the bullet holes to prove it (right).

dolphin. The original owner of what is now a grocer's shop at **Ashburton** in Devon incorporated spades, hearts, clubs and diamonds in the wall; inevitably it was known as the House of Cards. And when James Edward Elwell of **Beverley** built his half-timbered houses just outside North Bar – not in Tudor times, as they might appear, but in the 1890s – he decorated them with carved wooden replicas of Punch cartoons. One may not immediately get the point of the jokes, but then even Punch jokes have changed in the past 100 years.

Townsfolk have sometimes had their walls decorated whether they wanted it or not – even before the invention of the aerosol spray. The Civil War knocked a lot of walls down completely, but some remain which still bear their scars with pride. **Colchester**'s most famous battle was when Boadicea routed the Romans, but it was besieged during the Civil War too, and a building in East Street had its timbers riddled with bullet holes, which can still be seen. It is now a public house called, inevitably, the Siege House.

Although many old buildings have changed in their use, thoughtful owners have sometimes preserved a reminder of what they used to be. When a building society occupied the building at the corner of Norfolk Street and Surrey Street in **Sheffield** they retained the elegant inscription above the doorway, which recalls it was the Jeffie Bainbridge Children's Shelter. A local philanthropist, Emerson Bainbridge, built the Shelter in 1894 in memory of his wife, to provide homeless children with a roof over their heads. The present occupants also provide roofs over heads, but on a rather different basis.

Even when a building is demolished or drastically converted, some distinctive remnant of the original is occasionally retained. In another part of Sheffield, for instance, an old carved head has been attached to a new block of houses in Staveley Road. The head previously adorned the old houses that stood on the site.

This diligence on the part of the City Council is all the more commendable in that nobody is quite sure who this character is. It was assumed locally that as this was Staveley Road the head belonged to Lord Staveley. Indeed it is recorded that for many years passers-by doffed their hats to his lordship. But while 'Who's Who' has a Sir John Staveley, he was only knighted in 1980 and has lived all his life in New Zealand; Admiral Sir William Staveley was not knighted until a year later. I did have higher hopes of Martin Samuel Staveley CMG CVO CBE, whose address at first glance was Bradford, not too far away from Sheffield. At second glance, however, it turned out to be Bradford-on-Avon. So the bearded patriarch of Staveley Road keeps us guessing – but I raise my hat to him anyway.

Even supermarket chains can sometimes doff a hat to history. In **High Wycombe** the portico of the Old Red Lion Hotel with its red stone lion has been preserved as part of Woolworth's; it

Two Sheffield curiosities. A reminder of the Jeffie Bainbridge Children's Shelter (left) and the mystery man of Staveley Road (above). Nobody is sure who he was, but he still commanded the respect of passers-by. He has been preserved for old times' sake – and so has the Red Lion at High Wycombe, which now guards a supermarket instead of a pub.

THE
MARKET WEIGHTON
GIANT

THE FOOTPRINT
OF
WILLIAM BRADLEY
THE TALLEST
ENGLISHMAN EVER
RECORDED WHO LIVED
IN THIS HOUSE
BORN 10 FEB 1787
DIED 30 MAY 1820
HEIGHT 7FT 9INS
WEIGHT 27 STONES

ERECTED BY
MARKET WEIGHTON
CIVIC TRUST

More wall mementoes: the footprint of the Market Weighton giant (above) – the local pub still has his chair (above, right) – and the doorway of the original manor house which has been preserved by the supermarket which replaced it at Hungerford (below).

was here that Disraeli made his first election speech in 1832. And a High Street supermarket in **Hungerford** has retained the shape of a doorway (though not the doorway itself) which used to grace the eighteenth-century manor house on that site.

I vowed not to mention commemorative plaques, but the one on a cycle shop in **Market Weighton**, Humberside, is hardly the standard model. It depicts an enormous footprint, indicating that this was the home at the turn of the century of William Bradley, the Market Weighton Giant. The locals claim he was the tallest man ever born in Britain, and certainly he was a big lad; he was 7 feet 9 inches tall, his stockings measured 3 feet 9 inches (they must have come in very handy on Christmas Eve) and we even have the length of his inside leg, normally a secret between a man and his tailor – 5 feet 10 inches. His great size is all the more remarkable in that he was one of thirteen children, and the other twelve were all of normal height. His father was a mere 5 feet 9 inches, and his mother, who deserves our sympathy – William weighed 14 pounds at birth – was of normal size also, between pregnancies.

The footprint preserved at the cycle shop shows he took a 15-inch shoe, which was nearly 6 inches broad. The shoes themselves went to York Museum. He was reputed never to drink anything stronger than water, milk or tea, but the Londesbrough Arms in Market Weighton displays the chair in which he regularly sat, presumably to watch everyone else. The hotel also serves a 'Giant Bradley Grill', but William was a surprisingly moderate eater, so the dish should not overwhelm you.

Finally, if you lift up your eyes to the railway bridge which spans a street in **Lichfield**, Staffordshire, you will see a reminder of one of the grislier periods of early English history, the wholesale slaughter of Christians by the Romans under the emperor Diocletian. The very name Lichfield is said to originate from 'lych' field, the field of corpses, which was one of the products of Diocletian's purge, and on the bridge across St John Street is the city's seal, depicting the bodies of three kings who were among the Christians who defied the Romans and became the Lichfield Martyrs.

It is an indication of the singular failure of Diocletian's policy that the 'field of corpses' became the site of one of the finest cathedrals in England . . .

Lichfield's 'field of corpses', remembered on a railway bridge.

All Part Of The Service: Reading, Lighting And A-Grisly-Nick

A town's public services are not usually its most fascinating feature. Schools and libraries can be just blocks of glass and concrete, clock towers just something to tell the time by, a drinking fountain merely a pillar with a tap on it, a lamp-post is just a lamp-post. But there are exceptions. Schools and libraries can have their own unusual stories, clock towers can be historic monuments, fountains can look like Gothic castles – and how about a lamp-post which has a dog *on top*? As for a grisly nick, there are one or two still about – and prisons are part of the service too.

Libraries with church connections: Dr Plume's library (top) at Maldon was built on the side of a derelict church tower; the county library at Wymondham is in an ancient chapel.

People have been accumulating private libraries ever since Moses started collecting tablets, but it was not until 1850 here in Britain that the government passed the Public Libraries Act, which allowed a borough to levy a halfpenny rate to build a free public library. Until then people had to rely on the generosity of benefactors like Dr Thomas Plume of **Maldon** in Essex. Before his death in 1704 he built a library on the side of St Peter's Tower, all that remained of a ruined medieval church. It served as a grammar school on the ground floor, and above it he installed 7000 books.

Dr Plume bequeathed his library 'for the use of the minister and the clergy of the neighbouring parishes who generally make this town their place of residence on account of the unwholesomeness of the air in the vicinity of their churches'. Malaria was prevalent in rural Essex at the time and the clergy's devotion to their flocks apparently did not extend to living amongst them. Dr Plume himself spent much of his time south of the river as Archdeacon of Rochester, but he did not forget his home town.

His library still has a seventeenth-century flavour about it. with its fine old fireplace and its panelled walls. It is open to the public at certain times, though the volumes must be too valuable to be issued at the drop of a date-stamp. But conveniently the county library is now just below.

Dr Plume's choice of a site for his library has been emulated elsewhere in East Anglia, except that they have used redundant churches instead of ruined ones. The county library at **Wymondham** in Norfolk is housed in the ancient chapel of St Thomas à Becket, which has a history going back as far as its more prominent neighbour Wymondham Abbey. Indeed there have been stories of a tunnel connecting the two, but the holes which have occasionally been uncovered probably have a less romantic explanation – disused Victorian sewers.

The same sort of conversion happened to a Norman chapel on the outskirts of **Norwich**. It was originally the chapel of the Magdalen Leper Hospital, founded by

Norwich's first Bishop, Herbert de Losinga. At that time it was well outside the city, for obvious reasons. Since then Norwich has grown and leprosy has diminished, and the chapel has taken on a new role in a growing area of the suburbs.

Incidentally the straightforward conversion of a disused church into a library seems a kinder fate than the piecemeal changes that took place in **Richmond**, North Yorkshire. At one stage the main body of Holy Trinity Church was separated from the tower by an assortment of shops and offices. Happily it has now been sorted out more satisfactorily, and the bulk of the building has been converted into the regimental headquarters and museum of the Green Howards.

Two more churches pressed into public service. The chapel of the Magdalen Leper Hospital on the outskirts of Norwich is now a branch library (top); Holy Trinity Church in Richmond (above and left) was carved up into shops and offices and is now a regimental museum.

Can Midhurst claim to have the most attractive public library in the country? (above). Ross-on-Wye's Market House is another contender – not as old as Midhurst's Knockhundred Row, but it does have royal connections – a bust of Charles II and a carved heart bearing the initials FC (right) – not 'Charles loves Flossie' but 'Faithful to Charles in Heart'.

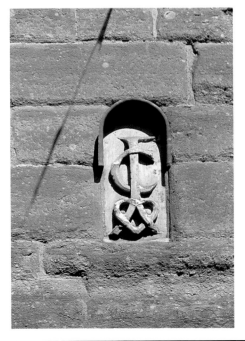

Meanwhile other towns and cities were finding homes for their libraries and museums in more secular surroundings. One of the most atractive public libraries in the country is at **Midhurst** in Sussex, a medieval house in Knockhundred Row with oak timbers and leaded windows. **Ross-on-Wye** makes use of a more dramatic building, the seventeenth-century Market House, built on fourteen arches and dominating the Market Place. The library is housed on the upper floor, behind the medallioned windows, the arched lights and the bust of Charles II on a white stallion between the gables, a reminder of the town's loyalty to the Royalist cause.

On another wall is a heart bearing the monogram 'FC', which might indicate that Charles dallied awhile in Ross-on-Wye with a Florence or perhaps a Fiona, but the loyal citizens prefer to interpret it as 'Faithful to Charles in Heart'.

If Midhurst and Ross-on-Wye are in the running for the most historic and attractive public library, where does one turn for the ugliest? I would hesitate to nominate **Stoke-on-Trent**, but even admirers of Stoke's library – and there must be some – would agree that it has some rather curious features. The windows on the top floor are reminiscent of a railway signal-box, while underneath is a row of massive circular windows with a layer of friezes in between. They feature a tiled portrait of Shakespeare, looking slightly dazed.

This was no conversion job but a brave attempt to make full use of that half-penny rate levied under the Public Libraries Act. They built a public baths too, but that was demolished some years ago and is now a car park. The library somehow survives.

For sheer size one has to admire **Manchester**'s circular central library, one of the biggest in Britain with a stock of nine million books. This also features a portrait of Shakespeare, this time in a stained glass window in the Shakespeare Hall and looking perhaps a little more relaxed than in the Stoke version.

The central library is an imposing successor to Chetham's library, founded in 1653, which Manchester claims to be

Stoke-on-Trent's astonishing public library (left), with signal-box windows round the top floor, massive portholes beneath, and a layer of friezes in-between. No wonder William Shakespeare, who is featured on one of the walls (below) is looking slightly dazed.

'Caxton', Bridgwater's unique library 'assistant' (above, right). It is a bookcase made out of an old printing frame. It is supposed to be a donkey but could also pass as a camel. The original school building at Winchester College (below) encouraged study, not with an eccentric bookcase but an illustrated Latin text (below, right).

the first free library in Europe, though Humphrey Chetham provided one in nearby Bolton at about the same time. The city also has the John Rylands Library with a world-famous collection of medieval jewelled bindings and historic writings going back to 3000 BC. It was endowed by a weaver's widow from Wigan in 1900 as a memorial to her husband. What with Mrs Rylands, Mr Chetham and the Public Libraries Act,

there must be enough reading matter available in the city for Mancunians never to turn on the television again . . .

Lastly on libraries, my favourite library 'assistant'. The name is Caxton, and readers welcome Caxton's help at **Bridgwater** library in Somerset. It is actually a bookcase made out of an old printing frame, said to be shaped like a donkey though it could just as easily be a camel, with type blocks   for teeth. It

AVT DISCE

AVT DISCEDE

MANET SORS TERTIA
CAEDI

was not around, unfortunately, when the Duke of Monmouth spent the night in Bridgwater before his disastrous defeat at Sedgemoor. It would have been nice to think that he took his mind off the morrow by browsing through Caxton's shelves.

The history of ancient libraries is often linked with schools. The great public schools are too famous to need mentioning – though it is interesting to find that a building at **Winchester** College, the original school, has an inscription in Latin on the wall which is rather more down-to-earth than the college's official motto, 'Manners Makyth Man'. The translation reads: 'Learn, Leave or be Licked'.

But there are historic schools and school buildings in our smaller towns which can be just as fascinating in their

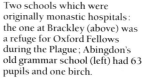

Two schools which were originally monastic hospitals: the one at Brackley (above) was a refuge for Oxford Fellows during the Plague; Abingdon's old grammar school (left) had 63 pupils and one birch.

own way as the Etons and Harrows and Winchesters. **Brackley** in Northamptonshire, for instance, not the most famous seat of learning, has Magdalen College School. It was originally a monastery, the Hospital of St James and St John, but in the fifteenth century it was bought by Magdalen College, Oxford so the Fellows could take refuge there during the plague. It has been a school ever since, with one of the oldest school chapels in the country.

Abingdon's old grammar school in Oxfordshire also started its existence as part of a monastic hospital. It had existed since before the Norman invasion; William the Conqueror left his son, the future Henry I, in the care of the Abbot. The abbey surrendered to an ungrateful descendant, Henry VIII in 1538, and 25 years later a wealthy City mercer called John Roysse bought the old Common Room of the Hospital for a not inconsiderable £50. Mr Roysse was 63 at the

Two more venerable schools: Market Harborough grammar school had a butter market underneath it (right), while the old school at Corsham had a splendid pulpit desk inside it (below and right). Ensconced in such an imposing vantage point, even the tiniest teacher must have felt like a lesser god.

time and the date was 1563, so he decreed that the schoolroom should be 63 feet long and accommodate 63 pupils.

It remained a grammar school until 1870, and the birch which was used on successive generations of 63 pupils is still on display. The room was used as a drill hall by the Abingdon Volunteers until it was renovated early this century and incorporated in the rest of the Guildhall, which is a splendid architectural mixture with every room built in a different period.

Market Harborough in Leicestershire has a half-timbered gabled building standing on wooden pillars which one might assume was the old market hall, but it was in fact another grammar school, founded in 1613. A butter market was held underneath, which could have been a little distracting for the children at their books above. Books and butter have both long since departed.

The old school adjoining the almshouses at **Corsham** in Wiltshire also stands empty, but the school furnishings have been preserved, dominated by the high pulpit desk where the master sat. It has a massive chair built into it, with high arms and a footrest; esconced in that, even the most dimunitive dominie must have felt like a lesser god.

Letchworth Garden City, by definition, cannot claim many historic establishments, educational or otherwise, but it does have a remarkable school building, the Cloisters, which was built as a school of psychology by an heiress called Annie Jane Lawrence. She arrived in Letchworth in 1905 and had the school built with a fountain and flooring in green-veined marble to represent spiritual growth. There was accommodation for twenty students in the cloisters. She lived to the age of 90 and liked to claim that in spite of her wealth she lived on 10 shillings a week, even in the 1950s. She might have been an interesting subject for her psychology students to study. But she actually outlived the school, which became a Masonic Lodge.

Life in public school, it is often said, can be excellent preparation for life in jail, and some of the buildings are not dissimilar. The earliest purpose-built prison in England is at **Hexham** in Northumberland, a grim edifice with narrow slit windows and 9-foot thick walls erected in the 1330s by order of the Archbishop of York, who obviously believed in dealing firmly with offenders. The first gaoler was a local barber, John de Cawode, who was paid twopence per day to look after his charges. This was not too arduous or dangerous a task, since they were kept chained and manacled. Hexham Prison remained in service for nearly 500 years, then it became the Manor Office, where manorial business was conducted. It must have provided a fitting atmosphere in which to pay the rates.

Before prisons were invented, the Druids had a more summary way of dispensing judgment and punishment. At **Llandudno**, high up on Pen-y-Dinas overlooking the town and the bay, there is a rocking stone which acted as judge and jury. The accused was blindfolded and told to place his finger on the only spot on the stone which would make it rock. If it did rock, he was innocent. If it didn't he was flung over the cliff.

Striking locations for study, correction and judgment. Greenveined marble for psychology students at Letchworth (far left), the earliest purpose-built prison at Hexham (left), and summary justice at Llandudno (above).

With the arrival of the English in Wales, stonemasons were too busy building castles to go in for jails, but **Beaumaris** got around to it in 1829, with the help of Joseph Hansom, mainly remembered as the inventor of the hansom cab, but quite an enterprising architect as well. Beaumaris Prison was only in use for 50 years, then the prisoners were transferred to Caernarvon, but you can still see how they lived, and worked, and in some cases died on the gallows.

It is the only prison to retain its treadmill in place. Prisoners sentenced to 'hard labour of the first class' spent 6 to 8 hours a day tramping on the wheel, six abreast. The wheel pumped water up to a supply tank, but there was no point in speeding up the pace to fill the tank and finish the stint, because the water merely overflowed back into the well to be pumped up again. Meanwhile the women prisoners had their own workshop underneath a nursery where their babies lay in cradles. A rope from each cradle dropped down into the workshop, so each mother could pull it and rock her baby to sleep without leaving her workbench. Mr Hansom had thought of everything . . .

Not all old prisons are quite so forbidding. The eighteenth-century jail at **Buckingham** looks rather like a cosy little castle, with ivy growing up the walls. **Thetford** in Norfolk has two old jails, the

Beaumaris Jail and its treadmill (above) were designed by the same man who invented the hansom cab. The stocks in the 'cage' at Thetford (right) on the other hand were a fairly standard pattern.

original 'cage' containing stocks in Cage Lane built in 1581, and a flint-walled town jail which replaced it in 1816. And a great many small towns have tiny lock-ups such as the Round House at **Castle Cary** in Somerset, which is only 7 feet across with a studded door designed for dwarfs. In case the purpose of these little buildings is not always clear, the one at **Swanage** in Dorset is plainly labelled:

> *Erected for the prevention of vice and immorality by the friends of religion and good order,* AD *1803.*

The Welsh had these lock-ups too. My favourite stands by the harbour at **Barmouth**, erected in the 1820s to accommodate not only drunken sailors but drunken goldminers who came down from the mountains to celebrate their latest 'strike'. The modest lock-up was Britain's only equivalent to the sheriff's cells in all those old gold-rush movies.

A number of old jails have finished up as just tourist attractions or tourist information centres, but **Bodmin** county jail has been turned into a restaurant. The sign by its imposing arched entrance no longer announces visiting hours but says invitingly: 'Parking Inside'. The diners can now be sure there are no files hidden in the cakes, and are presumably not put off

Village lock-ups were generally small and round with studded doors, like the one at Castle Cary (above). But sometimes they were small and rectangular with studded doors, like the one at Swanage (left). In case this confused people a plaque on the Swanage lock-up explained it was 'for the prevention of vice and immorality'.

Bodmin county jail is now a restaurant. The sign by the entrance no longer announces visiting hours but says invitingly: 'Parking Inside'.

their food by the thought that people were still being hanged there a little over a century ago. They can turn their mind to a happier memory: the Crown Jewels and the Domesday Book were concealed there during the First World War. It may have been chosen because Bodmin is the only town in Cornwall named in the Domesday Book – or perhaps it was just the least likely place to look for the Crown Jewels.

If it is a short step from public schools to prisons, the step from prisons to army barracks is even shorter. **Berwick-on-Tweed** claims to have the first barracks built in Britain – if one doesn't count the Romans. They were put up in the early eighteenth century when the locals objected to having soldiers billeted in the pubs. Nobody presumably asked the soldiers. The barracks, said to be the work of Vanbrugh, have quarters for other ranks and their wives which are not designed on his usual luxurious scale – they are more in the style of Joseph Hansom.

Civic authorities provided more congenial services than prisons; clocks, for instance. One of the earliest clock towers in Britain, completed in 1412, is at **St Albans** in Hertfordshire. It still strikes the hour on a bell which is even older than the tower. At **Swanage**, on the other hand, there is a clock tower without a clock. It started life at the southern end of London Bridge, as a memorial to Lord Wellington. Then the Metropolitan Police, without regard for his late lordship's feelings, declared it was an 'unwarrantable obstruction' and ordered its removal. It was snapped up by the Burt and Mowlem families, whose contracting business made it possible to acquire all manner of unwanted statuary, and they presented it to Swanage in 1867, along with other assorted masonry, mentioned elsewhere.

In due course local authorities also got around to providing a water supply. At **Cannock** in Staffordshire there is the Tank House, a six-sided building with a pyramid roof, where the town's first public water supply was brought by pipeline in 1736. It was built by the Cannock Conduit Trust, backed by the Lord of the Manor and the Bishop, and it served the town for 200 years. When it became redundant the city fathers felt it was worth preserving, even though it takes up valuable road space, and the double yellow 'no parking' lines have to swerve quite sharply to avoid it.

Biggleswade in Bedfordshire is just as proud of its more recent but much grander pumping station, New Spring Works. It is so grand in fact that it has been designated a listed building. Some say it has an ecclesiastical quality about it; glimpsed from the A1, if you dare take your eyes off the road, it looks more like a miniature castle. But everyone agrees, one thing it doesn't look like is a pumping station.

Having acquired a water supply many towns used it for another public service, to provide hydrants for fire-fighting – previously the local fire services consisted of a supply of leather buckets in the church porch – and drinking fountains. One of the earliest combinations of both must be the Fire Monument at **Blandford Forum**

in Dorset, disconcertingly known as Bastard's Pump; but that just happens to be the name of the man who provided it. John Bastard and his brother William were also responsible for most of the Georgian town we see today, because they were commissioned to rebuild Blandford after a disastrous fire in 1731 which destroyed most of the old wooden buildings – plus the old wooden fire engine.

Is it a castle, a cathedral, a monastery? No, it is a pumping station. Biggleswade's grandiose New Spring Works has been designated a listed building.

Cannock's Tank House is not so grandiose but much treasured nonetheless. It was the focal point for the town's first water supply and remained in service for 200 years.

With the money from a nationwide appeal, to which George II contributed 1000 sovereigns, they also rebuilt the Town Hall and the parish church, and of course the pump itself, just in case the town caught fire again – or as John Bastard put it, 'to prevent by a timely supply of water the fatal consequences of fire hereafter'. He also left enough money to keep the pump in repair and to pay for an oil lamp to be lit over it each night. The old pump was replaced by a fountain in 1895, when presumably the fire brigade felt they could cope without it. To show that John Bastard's public spirit is not dead, a notice announces that 'water is supplied gratuitously by Blandford Waterworks Company'.

The Gurney family of Norfolk has long been in the public spirit business, and John Henry Gurney took the trouble to erect a fountain in **Norwich** on the site in Tombland where pumping machinery was used between 1700 and 1860 'to raise and store the water supply for the higher parts of the city'. Noel Coward did not believe that Norwich could have any

higher parts – 'Terribly flat, Norfolk' – but if he had taken his driving test in the city and tried a hill start he might have thought again. Mr Gurney's fountain, alas, no longer functions, except as a litter bin. Perhaps a later generation of Gurneys will erect a new monument to replace the disused fountain which replaced the disused pump . . .

What do the Bastards of Blandford Forum have in common with the Gurneys of Norwich? They took a fancy to fountains. The Bastards' Pump was erected in memory of a disastrous fire and to ensure it did not happen again (above and right); John Henry Gurney's fountain was erected in memory of a pumping machine which served the city for 160 years (far right).

Before leaving pumps, you may be surprised to spot one in **Canterbury** which is half-way up a wall. This marks a very different kind of site. The pump is painted scarlet and it is here on the corner of Sun Street that a spring is said to have produced scarlet water – reddened by the blood of the murdered Thomas à Becket.

Fountains seem to bring out the worst in public behaviour. At **Salcombe** in Devon they have had to put up a notice warning that 'anyone found cleaning fish or erecting any other nuisance at this watering place will be prosecuted'. They also bring out the worst in architects. Some of the designs they conjure up are quite astonishing.

Perhaps the prize should go to the American Fountain in **Stratford-upon-Avon**, described by one of its kinder critics as 'a sort of squat, over-decorated clock tower with a fountain, two layers of pinnacles and a spire'. It has towered over Rother Market since Queen Victoria's golden jubilee in 1887, when it was unveiled by Henry Irving. It is not recorded what Mr Irving exclaimed when he saw it, but I can only note that the character who presented it to the town, George A. Childs, was an American from Philadelphia who did not have to live within several thousand miles of it.

A curious assortment of pumps and fountains. The scarlet pump in Canterbury (above, left) is a reminder of a murder; the fountain at Salcombe has a warning against misuse (below, left); and the American fountain at Stratford-upon-Avon (below) is an example of rather excessive generosity.

One of the earliest public baths was provided in Ditchingham (above) by an apothecary called John King. His subsequent essay, 'on Hot and Cold Bathing' might have made interesting reading in 1730. The Victorians, however, were not so risqué and concentrated their efforts on drinking fountains like this 'elaborate reincarnation of the Middle Ages' at Saffron Walden.

There is another Victorian concoction in the market place at **Saffron Walden** in Essex. If I may quote an independent witness again, 'it is as elaborate a reincarnation of the Middle Ages as only the Victorians could achieve, its squat columns and encrusted capitals heaped on each other in elaborate profusion.' There are also effigies in alcoves, gables, carvings and mouldings – and all just to provide a drink of water.

Some towns put their piped water supply to other uses for the general benefit of the townsfolk. One of the earliest public baths was provided in **Ditchingham**, near Bungay in Suffolk, by an apothecary called John King in about 1730. He must have spent many happy years studying the locals disporting themselves in his baths, because he published a document called 'Essay on Hot and Cold Bathing'. This might be a learned treatise or a sensational revelation – I am still trying to find a copy.

The first hint of civic street lighting comes in the seventeenth century. Records kept at **Bedford** town hall in the Black Book show that the householders in the High Street were ordered to hang out candles at night on a rota basis. The east side was lit on one night, the west side on the next. Revellers emerging after a long session could thus work out whether it was the same evening or they had lost a day, while courting couples no doubt arranged to meet on the unlit side.

Modern electric lighting offers less opportunity for romance, but in **Bungay** they have made use of an otherwise mundane lamp-post to recall a spectacular incident in the town's history. It involves a dog – so what better memorial than a lamp-post?

It stands near the Butter Cross, and on top of it is a weather-vane depicting a black dog with a lightning shaft beside it. This is Old Shuck, the fearsome Black Dog of Bungay, which appeared in the parish church during a thunderstorm and caused considerable mayhem among the congregation. A bronze plaque sums it up:

All down the church in midst of fire,
the hellish monster flew;
and passing onwards to the Quire
he many people slew.

A contemporary writer described how this horrific hound passed between two praying parishioners. 'It wrung the necks of them bothe at one instant clene backward, in so much that even at a moment, where they kneeled, they strangely dyed.' If you think this sounds a little fanciful I should tell you it was a clergyman who wrote it, the Rev. Abraham Felming. But I have to add that he was not actually there at the time.

The Black Dog of Bungay (above, left) once rampaged through a congregation but is now safely perched on a lamp standard. The Black Book of Bedford is still in the town hall (below, left) where it reveals how people managed before the lamp standard was invented.

Finally, another public service which has been around since the days of the post-chaise. There are still a few reminders of those early days of the postal service. For instance near the Old Town Hall at **Horsham** in Sussex there is a box let into the wall which bears the inscription,

Ye Olde Post Box of Horsham,

though it has now ceased to function and any letters posted in it will take even longer than usual.

Since that time we have grown used to those familiar red pillar-boxes on the street corners of our towns, and though the initials have changed over the years from VR to ERII the colour never varies –

Post boxes of the distant and more recent past. 'Ye Olde Post Box of Horsham' (far right) no longer functions, but you can still post air-mail letters in the blue pillar-box in Windsor (below).

except in Windsor. In 1911 the first letters to travel by airmail were flown from Hendon to Windsor Great Park; no great distance, but even so, one of the three planes which set out failed to make it. To acknowledge this modest milestone in aviation and postal history, **Windsor** has a special sky-blue pillar-box for airmail at the south end of the High Street, alongside a standard red model.

The authorities have not yet devised a system for transferring the letters direct from the blue box to the planes which constantly fly over it, in and out of Heathrow, so one might just as well post airmail letters in the ordinary one beside it. But where's the romance in that?

'LUXURY LINERS LADEN WITH SOULS'

Thus wrote W. H. Auden on cathedrals, and I hesitate to elaborate on such an elegantly-turned phrase. But luxury liners are not just notable for the passengers they carry. They are equipped with all manner of furnishings to make the voyage more interesting, they have some fascinating features in their design, and they sometimes carry curious cargo in their holds. When I visit our cities, these are the aspects of their cathedrals I try to explore – while recalling some of their odder 'passengers' too.

'To arrive at a cathedral city for the first time can be an unforgettable experience,' wrote that great cathedral connoisseur, Alec Clifton-Taylor. 'Nothing can ever quite equal the thrill of the initial impact.' And for me, no cathedral city has made a greater impact than **Norwich**, George Borrow's 'fine city', with that marvellous spire soaring above it.

Thanks to a well-known insurance society the spire is familiar to millions of people far beyond Norfolk, but they may not know that inside the cathedral the man who had it erected left another more discreet legacy. Bishop James Goldwell, who rebuilt the spire in the fifteenth century after the original was struck by lightning, put his pictorial signature in the presbytery. Each of the bosses in the roof bears his rebus – a gold well.

Not every Tudor bishop left such a pleasing mark on his cathedral. On the opposite side of Britain, on the far west coast of Wales, Bishop Barlow of **St David's** Cathedral had rather less respect for roofs. The story goes that he stripped the lead from the roof of the Bishop's Palace to pay for the dowries of his five daughters. If he had had more funds, or fewer daughters, the Palace might not be in ruins today. But he was not able to take away St David's status as a cathedral city, though it only has a population of 2000 people.

Its equivalent in England must be **Southwell** in Nottinghamshire, which has just 8000 people. The Minster was a collegiate church under York and was made a cathedral in its own right a hundred years ago. There is a reminder of its original function, as a collegiate church for secular clergy, in the corridor between the chancel and the chapter house. It is a carving of a secular cleric pulling both ears of a monk.

The spire of Norwich cathedral is familiar to millions (below, left) if only because of a certain insurance company, but the bishop who erected it left a lesser-known 'signature' inside the cathedral (below).

It is one of the many splendid carvings in the Minster which have impressed visitors ever since James I exclaimed: 'By my blude, this kirk shall jostle with York or Durham or any other kirk in Christendom.' It has a screen carved with nearly 300 figures, there is a man with toothache in the vestibule (he has a bandage round his face), and the master mason himself is represented in the chapter house, whose leaf carvings are the minster's crowning glory.

Two of the carvings which impressed James I in Southwell Minster.

Chelmsford has a cathedral and a population of 60,000, but is still struggling to achieve recognition as a city. This must irritate the city fathers (technically town fathers) since Chelmsford has been of some significance in Essex since Roman times. This was where the legions converged to cross the river on their way north to Colchester – and there has been a traffic jam at Chelmsford ever since. But the cathedral, which was only a parish church until 1914, is not quite in the same architectural league as the others in East Anglia.

It does however display one feature which the others cannot match. On an outer wall is the figure of St Peter, which in itself is not unusual. But this Peter is not draped in biblical robes, he is wearing the gear of a modern inshore fisherman, even down to the big rubber boots. St Peter is often depicted holding the key to Heaven, and this statue is no exception, but Heaven would seem to have a very modern security system, because he is holding a large Yale key.

There is a similar example of modern interpretation at another cathedral of fairly recent origin, in **Blackburn**. This was the home of James Hargreaves, inventor of the carding machine and the spinning jenny, which helped found the Blackburn clothmaking industry and the Industrial Revolution. The sculptor John Hayward bore that in mind when he created his massive portrayal of Christ the Worker over the door. The wrought-iron aureole which surrounds it is shaped like a loom.

Blackburn Cathedral's other striking feature is its font. It is shaped like an egg, with two figures on top, one kneeling, the other holding a cross. But alongside these modern additions some of the ancient trappings have been retained. When bishops arrive at the cathedral to be enthroned they still knock on the door with a Saxon hammer. The handle has been renewed but it still retains the original stone head.

That egg-shaped font is too new to have any legends attached to it, but the

Ancient disciple in modern dress at Chelmsford (above); ancient hammer and modern font at Blackburn (right).

broken eggshells in **Winchester** Cathedral commemorate a former bishop, St Swithun. It is a name you may only associate with weather forecasts, but in Winchester he is famous for the miracle of the eggs. Apparently a farmer's wife was on her way to market with a basket full of them when she was bumped into by a short-sighted monk, and dropped the lot. Bishop Swithun, instead of lecturing her on the folly of putting them all in one basket, miraculously made the eggs whole again, to the delight of the woman and no doubt the relief of the embarrassed monk.

So in St Swithun's shrine in the cathedral there is a broken eggshell at the base of each candlestick, which I find a lot more noteworthy than Winchester's more famous relic, the Great Bible, even though the Bible is valued some twenty million pounds more than the candlesticks.

Indeed there are a number of cathedrals where unusual little features like St Swithun's eggshells escape notice because of all the publicity given to more glamorous or expensive possessions. **Canterbury**, for instance, is famous among other things for its documents sealed by William the Conqueror, the wax funeral effigies of Edward II and Charles II taken from their corpses, the fourteenth-century effigy of Edward III carved so accurately that it shows how his fatal stroke made the side of his face droop; St Augustine's Chair, the Bell Harry Tower – all the stuff that cathedral guidebooks are made of. But how much more intriguing – and unique to Canterbury – is the water system installed by an ingenious twelfth-century prior called Wibert, who had a knowledge of hydraulics ahead of his time.

The key factor was the octagonal water tower just beside the cathedral, where water was fed in through leaden pipes from the Old Park Hills to the north of the city. From the tower it was distributed to all parts of the ancient Benedictine monastery. I like to think that Thomas à

Broken eggshells on the shrine of St Swithun in Winchester Cathedral (above, left) are a reminder of an early miracle; the water tower beside Canterbury Cathedral (above) is a reminder that saintly men could be practical too.

Hereford Cathedral is famous for its Mappa Mundi and its chained library (above) but just as remarkable to the industrial archaeologist are its splendid Gurney stoves (above, right).

Becket made use of that water to sluice himself down before his fatal encounter with Henry II's knights.

Similarly, **Hereford** Cathedral hogged the headlines with the controversy over the sale of its Mappa Mundi, and it is also famous for its historic chained library, but on a more basic level have you ever noticed those splendid Gurney stoves? Between the four of them they burn nearly ten thousand poundsworth of fuel a year, which is not the most economical way of heating a cathedral, but they are worth preserving and admiring as quite magnificent examples of industrial archaeology.

In **Exeter** Cathedral, if you look upwards, you will see the longest un-broken stretch of thirteenth-century Gothic vaulting in the world, and there is a rare minstrel's gallery and a bishop's throne made of oak without a single nail being used, so it was easily dismantled and hidden when Cromwell's men came on the rampage. But instead of looking upwards, look down, beneath the miseri-cord seats in the choir stalls. You will see a set of forty nine carvings, the earliest such set in England, which include, remarkably, an elephant.

There were not too many elephants wandering around Exeter in the thir-teenth century, so the woodcarver had no model to copy, and indeed he gave his elephant some rather eccentric feet, and tusks which look more like clubs. The theory is that it was based on the first elephant to be introduced into medieval England, a gift to Henry III from the King of France in 1253. Travellers from Lon-don did their best to describe it, and the carver made up the rest.

Exeter Cathedral's elephant has curious feet and tusks like clubs – but there weren't many elephants in Devon for the woodcarver to copy in the thirteenth century.

Two of Salisbury Cathedral's more unusual relics: the Boy Bishop, said to have been tickled to death – literally; and the brass plate marking the centre of the tower, after Wren found the spire was leaning off the vertical.

Salisbury is renowned for having the largest cloisters and the loftiest spire in England – the only spire loftier than Norwich. It has one of the four remaining copies of the Magna Carta and of course its medieval clock, the oldest in England and possibly in the world, which the statisticians say has ticked more than 500 million times. There is also the Boy Bishop by the west door, renowned not for ticking but for tickling – it was said the tickling was too much for him and he died laughing.

But a less well-known feature of the cathedral is the brass plate in the floor which is engraved: 'AD 1737: the centre of the tower'. It was put there after Sir Christopher Wren discovered that the spire was leaning nearly 2½ feet off the vertical. He straightened it with iron tie-rods, and happily when the rods were replaced in 1951 the spire had not budged.

I have one more example of a cathedral curiosity which may be overlooked amidst the more famous features. **York** Minster, the largest of England's ancient cathedrals and renowned for its stained glass, also has on a wall near the main entrance some ecclesiastical graffiti, written in Latin. The translation is an elegant tribute to the Minster:

As the rose is the flower of flowers, so this is the building of buildings.

One might add that the Minster's rose window, so magnificently restored after the 1984 fire, must surely be the window of windows . . .

A learned tribute to York Minster: *'As the rose is the flower of flowers, so this is the building of buildings'* (left).

Some cathedrals have a struggle to achieve the kind of international fame that York Minster enjoys. In **Chester**, for instance, that most historic of cities with its well-preserved city walls and its medieval pedestrian precinct called the Rows, the cathedral lost much of its character with the Victorians, who left behind only the misericords in the choir stalls. But it does contain an unlikely item which is worth a modest pilgrimage, a painting of the Madonna and Child on what looks like a spider's web.

The web actually comes from the ermine moth, and is slightly thicker and tougher. Even so, one wonders what prompted the artist to use such a fragile canvas. Could he not afford a real one? Was he plagued by ermine moths? Did he do it for a bet? And having painted it, who would want to buy it?

We only know that it came from the Tyrol, and the original painting of which it is a copy was in a church in Innsbruck. I gather quite a lot of web-painting went on in those parts at the turn of the

A familiar subject on an unfamiliar material in Chester Cathedral. The painting of the Madonna and Child is on the web of an ermine moth. It originated in the Tyrol at the turn of the eighteenth century; the Dean and Chapter have managed to keep it intact ever since.

eighteenth century, and presumably some English tourist brought this one home to decorate the cathedral. The Dean and Chapter must have found it a mixed blessing; it is so fragile it has to be kept in a special box with a light shining through it so it can be viewed without handling. But it is believed to be the only one in England and there aren't many left in the Tyrol, so Chester can claim a unique distinction. But I wonder if a cathedral really enjoys being renowned for a moth's web?

St Cuthbert of Lindisfarne was renowned for something more controversial – his dislike of women. After his body was brought to **Durham** and a cathedral built over his shrine, it was planned to build a Lady Chapel in the standard position at the east end of the cathedral. But they ran into so many structural problems the project was abandoned; they believed that St Cuthbert was expressing his disapproval. Thus Durham is the only cathedral in England with a Lady Chapel at the wrong end, by the west door.

St Cuthbert's influence spread beyond the Lady Chapel. Women were kept well away from his shrine and were only permitted in certain parts of the cathedral. There is a black marble slab in the nave, just east of the font, which they were not allowed to go beyond. If he were around today, it is not difficult to guess where St Cuthbert would stand on the ordination of women . . .

That is only one of the unusual features of his cathedral. During the battle of Neville's Cross in 1346, when the Scots were invading England, the monks sang mass on top of the tower to give the English forces moral support – from a safe distance. The abbot vowed that if the English triumphed, mass would be sung there on each anniversary of the battle. Happily he backed the winning side, and each year they still sing anthems from the tower. But the singing is only done on three sides; a chorister once fell to his death on the fourth side, and they will not risk it happening again.

A more grisly tale of sudden death is attached to **Canterbury** Cathedral – apart from the one involving Thomas à Becket.

The tower of Durham Cathedral, where anthems are sung each year to mark a victory over the Scots – but only on three sides.

The central figure was a servant woman called Nell Cook, who worked for one of the canons of the cathedral. She believed that her master was having an affair with her niece, and was so upset by this thought that she served both of them with a poisoned pie. The ecclesiastical authorities took a poor view of this, regardless of what philandering might have taken place, and the story goes that they buried Nell Cook alive beneath the paving stones of a passage which leads from the Infirmary Cloister to Green Court. Nell is said to have haunted that low arched passage ever since; certainly it is known locally as 'The Dark Entry'.

There is a fairly dark entry to the cathedral green at **Wells**, but happily there are no bodies buried beneath it. This is the gateway which leads into the market-place, and its local name is Penniless Porch because here lurked, not a restless spirit but penniless beggars, hoping to coax the odd coin from worshippers on their way to the cathedral.

Guildford Cathedral is too new to have such legends; it was only completed in the 1960s. Even so, it has already invested in a plaque to record its early days for future generations. While it was being built, services were held in the crypt under the Lady Chapel (at the east end of the cathedral – no problems with St Cuthbert in Guildford). At the top of the steps leading into the crypt is a piece of Jerusalem stone on which it is recorded that divine worship was conducted here between 1947 and 1961.

Before leaving Lady Chapels, a word about **Ely** Cathedral's. The most famous feature of the cathedral must be its central lantern on top of the octagonal tower; the oak uprights, each 63 feet long and 3 feet thick, are so heavy that on their route to the cathedral the roads and bridges had to be strengthened to take their weight, and hauling them up the tower must have been an engineering feat in itself.

The Penniless Porch outside Wells Cathedral, where beggars hoped to coax the odd coin from the congregation.

THIS JERUSALEM STONE WITNESSETH THAT THE CRYPT UNDER THE LADY CHAPEL WAS USED FOR DIVINE SERVICE FROM 1947 TO 1961

The Jerusalem Stone at Guildford Cathedral crypt, where services were held until the building was completed.

But having looked up to admire the lantern, look up also in the Lady Chapel and you will see the widest medieval vault in England. It has a span of 46 feet, yet the centre is only 13 inches higher than the sides. It is so delicately constructed, so they say, that it would not bear a man's weight. On my last visit the chapel was full of scaffolding; I hope they were keeping that warning in mind.

There can be no such fears with the massive arch that was erected in **Llandaff** Cathedral in South Glamorgan, spanning the nave. The cathedral was bombed during the last war and its reconstruction included this arch. It supports not just a man's weight but the weight of the cathedral organ. The builders have taken

no chances; it is made of reinforced concrete.

Finally, the 'passengers' in these luxury liners laden with souls. Cathedrals went in for a very good class of passenger – plenty of kings, bishops, statesmen, and the occasional genius. Westminster Abbey, the QE2 of cathedrals, has the pick of them, but some preferred a provincial interment.

King John, for instance, decided that he wished to be buried between the shrines of two saints in **Worcester** Cathedral, that magnificent backcloth to so many county cricket matches. Whether he thought he would absorb saintliness from St Wulfstan on one side and St Oswald on the other, or whether he just wanted to get a

Ely Cathedral's octagonal lantern has oak uprights so heavy that roads and bridges on the route to the cathedral had to be strengthened to take their weight.

Sir Francis Chantrey's 'Sleeping Children' in Lichfield Cathedral was greatly praised by the critics – and Sir Francis thought it was rather good too. It is said that he regularly returned to Lichfield to study his handiwork, hoping to gain further inspiration.

good view of the cricket, we may never know. But he left explicit instructions in his will, and there he lies beneath a tomb of Purbeck marble, the oldest royal effigy in England.

If you really have a taste for royal effigies, **Lichfield** Cathedral is the place. You will find them all over the west front, beneath two of the cathedral's three spires, the famous 'Three Ladies of the Vale'. Among the rows of statues, rubbing stone shoulders with apostles, saints and clerics, there are 24 kings of England, from William the Conqueror on. There are 113 statues altogether, nearly all of them put there by the Victorians – perhaps indeed by a Victorian hairdresser, as one critic unkindly suggested, 'since every little wisp of hair on every figure has been carefully set in a fussy little curl'.

For a more elegant example of the sculptor's art you can enter the doorway beneath this well-curled collection and head for Sir Francis Chantrey's 'Sleeping Children', two youngsters entwined rather uncomfortably in perpetual slumber. Not only the critics have praised it; Sir Francis thought it was pretty good himself. It is said he returned to Lichfield every year to sit in front of his handiwork, hoping to achieve further inspiration.

Cathedrals are not inclined to encourage facetious or even witty epitaphs for their 'passengers', unlike all those country churches where they are travelling steerage rather than first-class.

However there are one or two quirky ones about. **Ely** Cathedral has an ingenious poem in memory of an engine-driver and his fireman, William Pickering and Richard Edger, who died when the engine boiler exploded. Railway disasters seem to offer a special kind of inspiration to epitaph writers; you may well know the one that begins: 'My engine now is cold and still, No water doth my boiler fill'. But the writer of Messrs Pickering and Edger's memorial waxed far more lyrical. Here's a brief excerpt:

> *The line to heaven by Christ was made,*
> *With heavenly truth the rails are laid.*
> *From earth to Heaven the line extends,*
> *To life eternal where it ends.*
> *Repentance is the station then,*
> *Where passengers are taken in . . .*

It seems to be an earlier version in fact of Auden's metaphor about luxury liners, except these souls travel by train instead of ship.

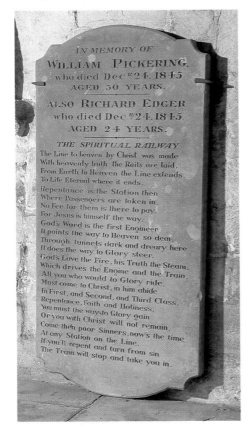

Cathedrals can be a little stuffy over epitaphs – they avoid the comical and the quirky – but Ely is rather proud of its memorial to an engine-driver and fireman who died in an explosion and departed this life on 'The Spiritual Railway'.

YOV SEE OLD SCARLETS PICTVRE STAND O'THE BVT AT YOVR ENTRE HERE DOTH HIS BODY LYE HIS GRAVESTONE DOTH HIS AGE AND DEATH TIME SHOW HIS OFFICE BY THEIS TOKENS YOV MAY KNOW & SECOND TO NONE FOR STRENGTH AND STVRDYE LIMB A SCARBABE MIGHTY VOICE WITH VISGE GRIM HEE HAD INTERD TWO QVEENES WITHIN THIS PLACE AND THIS TOWNES HOVSEHOLDERS IN HIS LIVES SPACE TWICE OVER: BVT AT LENGTH HIS ONE TVRNE CAME WHAT HEE FOR OTHER DID FOR HIM THE SAME WAS DONE: NO DOVBT HIS SOVLE DOTH LIVE FOR AYE IN HEAVEN: THOVGH HERE HIS BODY CLAD IN CLAY

The 'chief steward' who ushered passengers on board Peterborough's 'luxury liner laden with souls' to embark on their final journey. Robert Scarlett was the cathedral grave-digger; in his time he interred twice as many people as the total population of the city – or so the story goes.

I round off my 'passenger list' in **Peterborough**. There is little to commend the city itself; whatever the 'Peterborough effect' may be on the industries which are tempted there, it has had a pretty dire effect on Peterborough itself. But happily the cathedral has survived, with its three great archways over the entrances – why is the central one narrower than the other two, I wonder? – and its fine fan-vaulting behind the high altar.

Peterborough's most distinguished 'passengers' were Mary Queen of Scots and Catherine of Aragon, but also commemorated in the cathedral is the grave-digger who buried them. Robert Scarlett's epitaph notes that in his time he interred twice as many people as the total population of the city.

Not so much a passenger, was Mr Scarlett, more of a chief steward, ushering everybody else on board. May they all be enjoying a peaceful voyage.

I SAW MORE THAN SEASHELLS . . .

I have never had an urge to be a sailor. I share Dr Johnson's view of sea voyages: 'Being in a ship is being in a jail with the chance of being drowned'. But to quote a rather different source, 'I do like to be beside the seaside'. Great ports and tiny harbours have an equal fascination, not only to watch the boats come and go, the cheerful faces of embarking passengers and the greener faces of the returning ones, but also to explore the unusual maritime buildings and the stories that go with them, which can only be found within sight and sound of the sea.

My home port, if I can make such a claim without ever having sailed from it, is **King's Lynn**, fighting a constant battle to maintain access to the sea as the River Ouse lives up to its name, but still very active as the port closest to Birmingham and the industrial Midlands.

Its waterfront offers a fine assortment of curiosities. The seventeenth-century Custom House with its statue of Charles II was well-known to tourists even before it featured in 'Revolution'; the film was a disaster at the box-office but it made quite a profit for the residents of old Lynn, who cheerfully removed their cars, switched off their radios and put away their lawn-mowers to provide the right atmosphere for the film-makers, with no extraneous noises except the rustle of £10 notes . . .

Less photogenic but with a more unusual history is the building where the Registrar now keeps his records and conducts weddings. It was once the King's Lynn warehouse of the Hanseatic League. At school I used to confuse the Hansa with the Hausa and thought they came

Memories of the seafaring past in old King's Lynn. Hampton Court (above) still has the outline of the archways where ships tied up to unload, though the river has long since changed course; but floodboards are ready in case it returns. The Hansa warehouse (right) was built by Baltic merchants; it is now the Registrar's office.

from West Africa, but they were really a league of Baltic merchants who set up their own trading fleets and built three or four depots in England, of which only the one at Lynn still stands. The townsfolk, in the true Norfolk tradition, did not take too kindly to the foreigners who moved in, and were not above thumping them when the opportunity arose. They presumably took the view that Hansa needs a Boomps-a-daisy . . .

Thoresby College, a former college for priests just along the quayside, has a line across its central courtyard showing where the edge of the quay used to be before the Ouse changed its course; and there is more evidence at Hampton Court, a group of buildings well away from the water's edge, which still has the arches in its walls where ships tied up to unload. The river tends to return at times of flood, and propped beside each ground-floor doorway there is a flood board, ready to fend it off.

King's Lynn has one other feature connected with the quay that is worth seeking out. Behind a seventeenth-cen-

tury merchant's house there is an older tower, built of brick in Tudor times, five storeys high with a flat roof. This was the watch-tower where servants kept an eye open for the return of their master's ships.

Watch-towers are not unusual at seaports, but they are not always there for sighting ships. **Newquay** is best known these days as a holiday resort much

Another corner of old King's Lynn – the Tudor watch-tower (below) where servants watched for the return of their master's ships. Their master lived in Clifton House (below, left).

favoured by 'surfies' for its rolling Atlantic breakers, but it was once a fishing port specialising in pilchards. On Towan Head above the town there is the Huer's House, with its flight of steps leading up to the tower, where the huer – the look-out – would blow a horn when he sighted a shoal approaching. The house and its tower are painted a brilliant white these days and look as though they have been carved out of icing sugar, but they were far from just an ornament at the height of the pilchard season.

Whitstable in Kent also has a look-out tower, but you would hardly recognise it as such. It was used in the fifteenth century, not to spot pilchards or indeed the local oysters, but foreign invaders. In the last century, however, it was incorporated in a mock castle, which is likely to see just as little action as did the watch-tower.

There are two look-out towers on the beach at **Aldeburgh** in Suffolk which served a different purpose again. They were manned in stormy weather by two rival groups, the Up-towners and the Down-towners, in order to spot ship-

The Huer's House at Newquay (top) where a look-out kept watch for pilchards. And the watch-towers at Aldeburgh (above and right) where rival salvage teams kept a look-out for bigger game.

wrecks. The object was not entirely altruistic; there was as much interest in salvaging the cargo as succouring the crew. Even so, the race to get to the wreck first must have meant a better chance of survival for those on board, even if they lost their worldly goods in the process. If the Up-towners and Down-towners arrived at the wreck simultaneously and came to blows, might that be the origin of the up-and-downer?

Most coastal towers, of course, are designed less for look-outs and more for lamps. **Dover** claims the first lighthouse in Britain, built by the Romans in their fortress on the cliffs, now in the environs of Dover Castle. But somehow the idea didn't catch on, and it wasn't until the Tudors that we started building lighthouses on any sort of scale. In the interim the coastal towns enjoyed the fruits of the shipwrecks, and went in for a little wrecking themselves. Richard I was so annoyed he ordered that wreckers 'should suffer a rigorous and merciless death and be hung on high gibbets'. That was just for the rank and file; the ringleaders were to be 'tied to a stake in the middle of their own houses, which shall then be set on fire at all four corners, and be burned to the ground with all that shall be therein'. Powerful stuff; but then Richard, you will recall, had been shipwrecked himself . . .

Although there were no purpose-built lighthouses in the fourteenth century, a few kindly folk did display lights at their own expense for the benefit of passing ships, and the church lent a hand too. A number of medieval chapels on the coast were fitted with lights, and one of the few that survive is on Lantern Hill at **Ilfracombe**, the Chapel of St Nicholas. It had a projecting window on the seaward side in which the lantern was placed. The chapel became a house after the Reformation, but the light was still displayed, though on the roof gable instead of in the window. The light that hangs there now, surmounted by a weather-vane in the shape of a fish, was put there in 1819, about the time that Ilfracombe started developing from a small fishing village into a major holiday resort.

Early warnings for mariners. The Chapel of St Nicholas at Ilfracombe, now a private house, displayed a lantern in medieval times, and the tradition continues (top). But the first lighthouse in Britain was much earlier than that, built by the Romans at Dover (above).

When lighthouses came into more general use many of them were still owned and operated privately. Among the earliest were the High and Low Lights at Harwich. They were originally wooden structures owned in 1801 by a Mrs Rebow of Colchester. They were replaced in 1818 by the two towers which stand there today, but they stayed in the Rebow family until Trinity House took them over in 1836. They have not been used for over a century; one has been restored as an exhibition piece, the other is a museum. But there has recently been a reminder of their original owner.

According to Trinity House records Mrs Rebow was the only woman lighthouse owner in the country, a distinction

An assortment of early lighthouses at Harwich (right, and opposite page). They were originally privately owned until Trinity House took over.

which it has taken nearly 200 years to match. Trinity House has agreed to hand over their lighthouse at **Happisburgh** to a Trust, making it the only privately-operated lighthouse in Britain – and the leading light in the Lighthouse Trust is a woman. So the wheel has turned full circle – and thanks to the Trust, the light will continue to do that too.

(I agree Happisburgh is too small to qualify as a town, but a burgh is the next best thing – and it's a nice story.)

While enterprising lighthouse entre-preneurs like Mrs Rebow were making money out of protecting ships, port authorities were making money out of handling them. In the days before con-tainerisation, back in the 1820s, the port of **Goole** used Tom Puddings on much the same principle. A Tom Pudding was an iron tub, in effect a container with an open top, which could hold 35 tons of coal. They were filled at the South York-shire mines further up the Humber, and floated downstream to Goole, linked together and towed by a tug.

When they reached the docks the operation then differed from the modern version. Instead of being loaded directly

The Tom Puddings of Goole (below) carried coal down the river from the coalfields to the docks. They were turned over and emptied into a ship's hold – like emptying a pudding on to a plate.

on to the ship, they were raised on a hoist, turned upside down, and emptied into the ship's hold – like a pudding being turned out on a plate. Tom Puddings were operating in this way until 1986. Today Goole still handles coal, but most of it is coming in the opposite direction.

An even older loading device has been preserved on the Green at **Harwich**. The town's naval connections go back to 1340, when Edward III's fleet gathered in the anchorage before setting sail to fight

The treadmill crane at Harwich (above) was used to load ships by legpower in the days of Charles II. By the time the harbour-master's office at Holyhead was built (right) mechanisation had arrived, and Telford erected a Doric portico (below) to mark the triumphal completion of his road from London.

the first sea battle in what turned out to be the Hundred Years' War. They set off in great spirits; if they had known it was going to last that long, they might not have been so cheerful.

The treadmill crane on the Green does not go back quite that far, but it has been in the town since the seventeenth century when Samuel Pepys, as well as writing diaries, had a day job as Secretary of the Admiralty. He was also MP for Harwich, which might explain why quite a number of naval ships came there for victualling. The treadmill crane, using leg power in the same way as the prison variety but to rather more useful effect, loaded the ships with stores and ammunition. It may also have loaded a few sweetmeats and a case of claret on board the boat which took Charles II on the first pleasure cruise from the port of Harwich.

Supervising all these goings-on at Goole, Harwich and elsewhere were the harbour-masters and port authorities, bodies of considerable importance and often with offices to match. Some of these buildings have now seen better days. The port office at **Penarth**, for instance, which once supervised the loading of 4 million tons of coal a year, has been converted into a hostel, while the neo-Classical office at **Barry** is surrounded by docks which are mostly empty and marshalling yards which are mostly unused.

Further along the South Wales coast the port office at **Cardiff** was so imposing that one ecstatic visitor wrote: 'It stands bold as a castle, luxurious as a mansion, still polychromatic with stained glass windows, still fragrant with its old mahogany, still to be seen like a major-domo on its waterfront greeting its twenty or so ships a week ...' Alas, I gather this portside palace is no more, but I thought such pulsating prose was worth another airing ...

The harbour-master at **Holyhead** does not have quite such a polychromatic headquarters, but he does have a Doric portico reminiscent of the great arch which used to stand outside Euston station. It marks the end of Telford's road from London for travellers taking the ferry to Ireland.

The harbour office at **Lymington** in Hampshire also has an unusual neighbour. Adjoining it is a narrow white-painted building with a big bay window; it boldly displays the name, Pressgang Cottage. This was where the local press gang had its headquarters, in the days when Lymington rivalled Southampton and Portsmouth in importance. One wonders whether they had a working arrangement with the harbour-master next door.

Lyme Regis harbour also used to be much busier; the Duke of Monmouth considered it important enough to land there when he started his rebellion. Then things fell away. Would the town have done better, I wonder, if it had kept the name it chose first when Edward I granted its charter: King's Lyme? Perhaps they thought it might be confused with that other port in Norfolk, or maybe it sounded too much like a royal fertiliser. Either way, its royal connection failed to preserve its maritime importance, and the harbour came to be mainly used as a market. An early list of harbour dues is still on display: 1s 6d for a front stall, a shilling for a rear one, sixpence to park a brush or hardware van. There is no record of what they charged in more recent times for parking The French Lieutenant's Woman on the harbour wall, but I suspect it was more than sixpence.

The Cinque Ports might be considered oddities in themselves, since only Dover remains a port of any significance. Others have silted up or the sea has receded; as ports, four of the original Cinque have sunk. But **Hastings** still has a lively fishing industry, and the boats are brought ashore at the Old Town alongside the tall, narrow, wooden towers which stand above the high-water mark. These are the net huts, dating back to the sixteenth century. They are tall and narrow because the fishermen had to pay ground rent on whatever space they occupied, so they built upwards instead of sideways.

The lofts stand three storeys high, black, windowless and rather forbidding. A number were burned down in a fire in 1961 but were replaced in their original style and are still in use. The fishermen's

Reminders of earlier maritime days. Pressgang Cottage at Lymington (above) was conveniently next to the harbour-master's office; the table of charges on Lyme Regis harbour (left) requests sixpence for parking a brush or hardware van.

The net lofts at Hastings (right) are still used by the fishermen, but Padstow harbour (below) lost much of its trade because of a vengeful mermaid.

chapel nearby is also still used on occasions, though it is primarily a museum. The font remains, and fishermen's children can still be baptised in it. The pulpit was installed on the museum's main exhibit the *Enterprise*, the last vessel to come out of the Hastings shipyard before it closed early this century. It has been the practice to hold a harvest festival service there, the parson going on board the *Enterprise* to preach, safe in the knowledge that in its case a Hand *hath* bound the restless wave.

Among other towns which have lost their importance as ports over the years, spare a special thought for **Padstow**, which still has a delightful little quay but lost its deep water harbour in strange circumstances. Legend has it that a mermaid was bathing in the harbour, as mermaids will, when a local resident, perhaps thinking he had spotted a sexy shark, took a pot-shot at her. Understandably she was much put out by this and placed a curse on the harbour, in particular on a sandbank which has caused many shipwrecks since and is known as Doom Bar. She may have altered the composition of the sandbank in the process, because in the nineteenth century it was found to contain a high proportion of carbonate of lime, much valued as a fertiliser, but that was small compensation for losing the shipping trade.

However Padstow can claim one minor record, perhaps as a result of the mermaid's displeasure. Until 1952 it had the biggest lifeboat in Britain; the list of shipwrecks on the North Quay explains why . . .

MR MAYOR, I BEG TO MOVE ... INTO A NEW TOWN HALL

In the beginning there was the Tolbooth, just a roof on wooden posts where they collected the market tolls. When the city fathers needed a room to meet in, they built it over the Tolbooth to avoid occupying valuable renting space on the market itself. Thus the Tolbooth begat the Town Hall, with the council chamber upstairs and an open area beneath. This in turn begat the ostentatious city halls of the Victorians and sprawling civic centres of today, where the only similarity with the draughty old Tolbooth is that this is where you pay your rates – and feel another sort of draught as a result. Fortunately many links with those more colourful days remain, and even some of our more recent town halls have strange tales to tell.

When the Victorians decided to indulge themselves with a new town hall, mercifully they did not always destroy the old one. In places such as **Leominster** it is therefore possible to see how a town hall used to look, and what the Victorians turned it into. Their architects seemed to revel in the Italianate, the Gothic, the Baroque, or the just plain ugly. In Leominster they plumped for standard nineteenth-century Italianate – about as far as they could get from the traditional timbers of the original town hall, built in 1633, which they sold for a modest £95. It was moved bodily from its central position on the main crossroads to a less prominent site, and renamed Grange Court.

It doesn't look quite as it did before; the oaken colonnades at ground level, where the butter market used to be held, have been filled up with masonry. But the original carvings on the upper walls remain, and so does the inscription on the frieze which says the wooden columns support the building 'as noble gentry support the honour of a Kingdom'.

Two examples of traditional town halls, Leominster's has been moved bodily from its original site and the ground floor colonnades have been closed up, but overall it looks much the same as when it was built in 1663 (above). Bridgnorth's was built about 20 years later and has never budged; those massive legs were not made for walking (below).

The supporting columns of **Bridgnorth** town hall, made of sandstone and later covered with brick, have not budged since they were built in 1652. The money came from a nationwide appeal after most of the town was burnt down during the Civil War. When improvements to the building were needed ten years later, Charles II himself organised a whip round, in gratitude for the town's loyalty to the Crown. He ordered a collection to be made in every parish in England – an early forerunner of the Archbishop of Canterbury's urban appeal fund.

Even so, the builders had to exercise certain economies. Timbers for the upper storey were acquired from a ruined barn at Great Wenlock for about fifty sovereigns. Later they picked up the clock, which has dials at each end of the hall, for a modest £8.

Abingdon town hall is still called the County Hall, a reminder that when it was built in 1678 Abingdon was the county town of Berkshire. A boundary change has since moved it – no doubt kicking and screaming – into Oxfordshire. The building was designed to have three uses

instead of the usual two. In addition to a meeting room over an open market there were spacious cellars provided for use as a warehouse. As it turned out, the roof came in handy as well. On days of national rejoicing, like the Queen's Silver Jubilee and the Queen Mother's eightieth birthday, the town councillors follow the tradition of going on the roof and throwing down buns to the populace below. In the early days, when buns were a luxury for many, there was quite a struggle to catch them – and thus the 'bunfight' was born.

Occasionally a Victorian architect would control his urge to build a municipal castle and follow the tradition of combining the town hall with the market. **Cardigan's** Guildhall was built in 1859 to incorporate a covered market on the ground floor, where stalls could be erected underneath arches around a cen-

tral quadrangle. There is even a basement with more arches to take the overflow. The whole effect is a little monastic, but at least he had the right idea.

On the other hand **Birmingham** town hall looks as if it ought to stand on a Greek hillside, instead of within shouting distance of New Street Station. It was in fact modelled on a building in ancient Rome, and the city fathers were so delighted with it they chose it as the winning entry in a competition for their new headquarters. The successful architect was Joseph Hansom, a versatile fellow who also designed Beaumaris Jail. However, he bit off more than he could chew with this colonnaded monster; he ran into money trouble with the builder and ended up virtually bankrupt. It took seventeen years for the building to be completed, and by that time Mr Hansom was back in London designing cabs.

Birmingham town hall, which with Beaumaris Jail proved that Joseph Hansom could design very large buildings as well as quite small cabs. It might look more appropriate on a Greek hillside than within shouting distance of New Street Station, but the city fathers must have liked it – they awarded it first prize in their competition.

Municipal marvels in the West Country: the 'hotch-potch of baroque styles' at Tiverton (below) and the façade acquired from the Mercers at Swanage (below, right).

The Victorian enthusiasm for giving a foreign flavour to our civic buildings ranges from the Florentine grandeur of Bradford's massive city hall to the smaller but highly elaborate town hall at **Tiverton** in Devon, built in what one expert described as 'a hotch-potch of baroque styles with more than a dash of French dressing around the roof'. An unusual exception is at **Swanage** in Dorset, where the 1883 building acquired a seven-teenth-century stone façade designed by Christopher Wren, which came from the front of the Mercers' Hall in the City of London. It was a gift from the Burt and Mowlem families, who ran an up-market building and demolition business and got hold of all manner of cast-off masonry. The clock tower in Swanage, mentioned in another chapter, was also a product of their superior salvage operations.

Once the architect had completed his town hall, whatever style he had chosen, he often stuck something symbolic on top, to round it off. In this he did follow earlier tradition, since town halls have always provided a useful setting for a statue, or a bell, or more usefully a clock. It happened at least as far back as the fourteenth century. **Lincoln**, for instance, has a Mote Bell on the roof of its old Guildhall which is claimed to be the oldest of its kind in the country. It bears the date 1371, and they still ring it on special occasions.

At the other extreme the relatively new town hall at **Kendal** has a carillon in its tower which plays English, Welsh, Scottish and Irish tunes – mercifully only six times a day. To ensure there is no bias, the tunes are played on a rota basis, with each country allotted a different day.

The Victorian architect who designed the town hall at **Kingsbridge** in Devon added an onion-shaped clock tower to give a dash of excitement to what otherwise looks a fairly humdrum building – though behind that modest façade there is not only a civic office but a theatre, a cinema and a market.

Colchester town hall, on the other hand, does not attempt to conceal its vastness. It dominates the High Street, with not just a clock in its tower but a statue above the clock. It depicts St Helena, daughter of King Cole, who according to legend must have led a very full life and produced a very remarkable family. It is said he founded Colchester as well as his famous string trio, and he also fathered the Roman Emperor Constantine.

Others, however, argue that Constantine was born in York, his father was the Emperor Constantius Chlorus, and 'fair Helena of York' was not his sister but his mother. Perhaps it was confusing the historians that made King Cole so merry. But that is certainly Helena on top of Colchester's clock tower, bearing a sceptre and cross and facing, not York, but Jerusalem.

Crowning glories: Kingsbridge's onion-shaped clock tower (left) and Colchester's lofty statue of St Helena, daughter of King Cole (above).

Assorted ornaments: Sheffield town hall has a Vulcan at the top (right) and an owl and pelican on the walls (above). Worcester's Guildhall has Charles I and II beside the entrance (below, right) and Cromwell pinned by his ears inbetween (below).

Other town halls keep clear of nursery rhymes and stick to mythology. Felix Rossi's statue of Minerva on **Liverpool** town hall is perhaps the most famous example, Vulcan on **Sheffield**'s clock tower perhaps the most appropriate. He was chosen by the steel city as he was the god of fire and metalworkers. The naked figure looks tiny from ground level but it stands 7 feet high and weighs 18 hundredweight. The story goes that it was modelled on one of Queen Victoria's lifeguards, though it is difficult to imagine that prim lady allowing one of her soldiers to display himself so brazenly.

The statue is only one of the town hall's adornments. Vulcan appears again in company with Thor (another guardsman, or perhaps John Browne?) over the front door, and on a frieze along the front of the building there are representatives of all the city's arts and trades, from silversmiths to smelters. When an extension was built in 1923 two more carvings were added, an owl and a pelican. A guidebook explains, somewhat sycophantically, that they represent the wisdom and intelligence of the city council. That covers the owl, but a pelican's main attribute is its very large mouth . . .

The figures carved on **Worcester**'s Guildhall are much older, but present a much more unequivocal picture. There are statues of Charles I and Charles II on each side of the main door and between them, above the doorway, is a head nailed to the wall by the ears. The ears are so large and pointed one might think one was back among the Vulcans again on Star Trek, but this is supposed to be the head of Oliver Cromwell, not Mr Spock, nailed there as an indication of Worcester's loyalty to the two kings. Queen Anne also lurks between the two central windows, and for good measure there are five statues above the cornice representing Justice, Peace, Plenty, Chastisement and – the odd man out – Hercules.

Braintree town hall in Essex has only one of the virtues depicted on it, but it was not built until the 1920s when perhaps virtues were in short supply. Its dome is crowned with the bronze figure of Truth, a reminder of the town motto, 'Hold to the Truth'. The building with its central tower and five-belled clock did not have to be paid for by the ratepayers, it was a gift of the Courtauld family, whose silk mills at one time employed over 3000 local people.

Stow-on-the-Wold town hall in the Cotswolds has a statue of Edward the Confessor over the door, an unusual subject for civic statuary. He was presumably linked with the parish church, which is dedicated to St Edward. However, the statue is not the most unusual feature of the hall. The cost of building it, just over £4000, again did not fall on the ratepayers; in this case it all came from the unclaimed deposits in the local savings bank. If any claimant arrived subsequently, his only satisfaction was the knowledge that his deposit might have paid for a small portion of King Edward.

It is quite common for a town hall to have a clock, or a weather-vane, or both, but the old town hall at **Evesham** has a wind indicator, a thermometer and a barometer as well. This meteorological cornucopia was the gift in 1886 of the Rev. George Head of Aston Somerville, a cleric obviously much preoccupied with the weather. The wind indicator used to

be connected to a weather-vane on the roof, but that has now been taken down.

Rochester Guildhall also lost its weather-vane. This was a much more elaborate affair in the shape of a full-rigged ship made of copper and 5 feet

Stow-on-the-Wold town hall has Edward the Confessor over the door, an unusual subject for civic statuary (below).

The old town hall at Evesham eschews statuary in favour of meteorology; it is adorned with a wind indicator, thermometer and barometer, presented by a cleric who, like so many Englishmen, was much preoccupied with the weather.

A gruesome form of civic regalia. Leicester Guildhall still houses a set of gibbet irons last used in 1832 (above).

Rye town hall goes a stage further; it has preserved not only the gibbet but the last skull to occupy it (left).

long, a symbol of the town's nautical heritage. Alas, the ship could not reef its copper sails during the great gales of October 1987 and was blown down.

What does survive at the Guildhall, however, is a reminder of a gallant sailor who came to a very strange end. The moulded ceiling in the council room was the gift of Sir Cloudesley Shovell, who like Nelson was born in North Norfolk and became an admiral, but also went into politics and became MP for Rochester.

Sir Cloudesley was sailing past the Scillies on his way home from the wars when he had a disagreement with his pilot and hanged him from the yard-arm. This proved a little over-hasty, since nobody else knew the route, and the ship promptly ran aground and sank. While most of his unfortunate crew drowned the admiral managed to struggle ashore. He encountered a woman on the beach and asked the way to the nearest officers' mess. Following the tradition of Cornish hospitality to shipwrecked mariners in the seventeenth century, she thumped him over the head and stole his emerald ring. Sir Cloudesley, already weakened by his long swim, was in no state to defend himself and forthwith expired, whereupon his assailant buried him nearby and went on her way with the ring, rejoicing. It was 30 years later, when she confessed on her deathbed, that other shovels uncovered Sir Cloudesley and he was transferred to Westminster Abbey.

The admiral's untimely end is just one of the strange stories which come to light once one starts delving into our town halls. Many local authorities have preserved curious relics in them with just such delving in mind. There is for instance the set of gibbet irons in **Leicester** Guildhall. The last man to occupy them was James Cook, who murdered a commercial traveller for his money, then cut up the body and attempted to burn it in his bookbinder's shop in Leicester. Rashly he went out while the remains were still smouldering, and the chimney caught fire. He returned to find a crowd had gathered, attracted not only by the smoke but by the strong smell of burning flesh.

Cook claimed optimistically that he was merely cooking meat for his dog, but a doctor was called and identified the flesh as human. The murderer made a run for it, got as far as Cheshire and was actually boarding a ship when he was caught. He was hanged before a crowd of 30,000 people in 1832, and was left to dangle in the gibbet irons until no doubt his own flesh was in even worse shape than his victim's.

Rye town hall in Sussex has preserved not only a gibbet but the skull of one of its occupants, a butcher called Breads. The bizarre feature of Breads' story – if gibbet and skull were not bizarre enough – is that he was hanged for killing the wrong man. He intended to kill James Lamb, mayor of Rye and owner of elegant Lamb House. Somehow he managed to murder Lamb's brother-in-law, Allen Grebell, instead. The unlucky Mr Grebell is said to haunt Lamb House, which later became the home of the novelist Henry James, but there are no reports that Butcher Breads has returned to the town hall to retrieve his skull.

The Shire Hall in **Warwick** offers a more comprehensive reminder of medieval justice. Beneath it is a dungeon, shaped rather like an underground beehive. There are eight posts in a circle on the floor, each with a staple through which a chain was passed, and this chain was threaded through the manacled legs of the prisoners. They were often packed in so tightly that there was only room to lie on their sides. In the centre of this circle of recumbent bodies was a drain, which looks like a primitive form of sanitation, but it had the additional use of draining away the water when the dungeon was flooded, a not infrequent occurrence. The chain through the prisoners' legs continued up the stairs through an inner door and was then padlocked to the wall outside; there are still the grooves on the stairway where it rubbed against the steps.

The dungeon was constructed in 1680 and was in use for over a hundred years. During the Stuarts it was mainly occupied by Quakers, Anabaptists and other 'unorthodox folk'. Then it was used for

Army deserters until John Howard, founder of the Howard League, had it closed down in 1797. The plaque which tells its story is becoming something of an antique in its own right; it bears the date 1932.

The Shire Hall in Warwick contains a more comprehensive reminder of medieval justice, the dungeon in which prisoners were manacled in a circle around a hole that provided flood drainage as well as sanitation.

Early records at Bedford (right); and an even earlier roof at Exeter (below), 'the oldest Municipal Hall and Criminal Court in the Kingdom'.

A number of town halls preserve stocks and whipping posts, but **Congleton** in Cheshire goes one better with a brank, or scold's bridle, a collar with a chain on it which was used to attach nagging wives to a wall in the market-place. There is also a leather belt with a rather happier history. It has three bells hanging on it called St Peter's chains, and on the eve of St Peter's Day it was the custom for a priest to dance around the town, ringing the bells. Originally this was a pagan ceremony to ward off evil spirits, but later it acquired a different meaning – it meant that chimney-sweeps could take a day off.

In case you wonder how a chimney-sweep would hear the bells if he was up a chimney at the time, the solution may lie in the records of the town officers, which are also preserved at the town hall. These officers include an ale-taster, a swine-catcher and a chimney-looker. Presumably it was his duty on St Peter's Day to look up chimneys and ensure nobody was working overtime.

The old records kept at **Bedford** town hall also set out the duties of the town officers, including the municipal cowherd. He had to blow his horn each morning to warn the townspeople to bring him their cows, so he could take them out to pasture. When he brought them back in the evening he blew it again, so the owners knew when to collect them.

Exeter's Guildhall goes back a lot further than that. It is claimed to be 'the oldest Municipal Hall and Criminal Court in the Kingdom', and since Exeter is one of the oldest cities in the kingdom, founded by the Romans in AD 50, it has reasonable grounds for saying so. The Guildhall's foundations may not go quite as far back as that, but they were probably laid by the Saxons and were certainly there in Norman times. It was rebuilt in 1330, the roof work and panelling is fifteenth century, and the arched front was added in Elizabethan times, when most of our old town halls were just about getting started.

Scunthorpe municipal centre was only built in 1963, but it does incorporate one feature which is even older than Exeter's.

Built into the wall of the entrance hall is a section of mosaic pavement from a Roman settlement at Winterton, 5 miles away. The Romans came and went in Scunthorpe some 1600 years before British Steel did much the same thing.

Many civic authorities like to remember their towns' past by displaying portraits or busts of famous citizens; **Durham** prefers to display a set of clothes. They belonged to Count Joseph Boruwlaski, who was born in Poland in

Scunthorpe Municipal Centre was only built in 1963 (top) but it contains a 1600-year-old mosaic from Scunthorpe's Roman days. The section of pavement has been built into the wall of the entrance hall (below).

Strange figures in civic surroundings: 'Lord Tom Thumb' – with some of his wardrobe – keeps a nonchalant eye on things at Durham (above and above, right), while a freed slave and a bare-breasted lady stand guard at Kettering (right).

1739 but spent the last 17 years of his long life – he was 98 when he died – in Durham. He was an accomplished violinist, and his violin is there with his suit, gloves and cane, but that was not the main reason for his fame. The Count stood only 39 inches high; he has gone down in history as Lord Tom Thumb.

Kettering town hall has an unusual reminder of the locally-born missionary William Knibb in its coat of arms, which was redesigned when five local authorities became a single borough in 1974. Mr Knibb does not feature in the design himself, but his pioneering work for the abolition of slavery is represented by a black man with a broken chain around his wrist – and wearing, it would seem, a pair of blue swimming trunks to preserve the decencies. The figure opposite him appears a lot more brazen – a buxom, bare-breasted lady with skirt daringly cut to the thigh. Is there some romantic link between the two? Alas, the twain never met. The lady originates from the coat of arms of the Dukes of Buccleugh, whose family was linked with the ancient Manor of Kettering. Nothing for the *News of the World* there . . .

While there is a logical explanation for featuring an African slave in Kettering, it is not so easy to understand why two eighteenth-century ships' cannon are guarding a town hall in land-locked Surrey. **Leatherhead** is a long way from the sea, and is not generally associated with naval battles against the Spanish,

but the cannon were captured in 1762 by the British fleet at the Battle of Havana, and somehow found their way in due course to Leatherhead town hall.

Similarly it is disconcerting to find **Pontefract** old town hall in Yorkshire housing the original plaster cast for one of the panels on Nelson's Column in Trafalgar Square. But there it is, with the dying Nelson being carried through the thick of the fray. A sailor is firing a gun over Nelson's head while resting one foot on the head of a recumbent comrade, who in turn is resting his head on the knee of somebody else; they obviously have more things to worry about than an expiring admiral. But there is no doubt what is going on; the panel bears Nelson's farewell cry, 'They have done for me at last, Hardy.'

No mistaking who the casualty is here; the dying Nelson is being carried through the thick of the fray at Trafalgar. But this plaster cast for one of the panels on Nelson's Column is nowhere near Trafalgar Square – it decorates Pontefract old town hall.

The panelling in the assembly hall at **Swansea** civic centre has also travelled a long way. It was designed by Sir Frank Brangwyn for the House of Lords, as a memorial to the peers who died in the First World War. He worked on it for 7 years, only to have it turned down by their lordships as being too gaudy. One unkind critic described the panels as 'the largest postage stamps in the world'.

Sir Frank, understandably irritated, offered them to his friend Sir Percy Thomas, who happened to be the architect for Swansea city hall and law courts, and he redesigned the hall to accommodate them. Since then they have been described as 'nothing short of a stunning achievement, a brilliant combination of superb pattern-making and assured draughtsmanship.' So much for critics . . .

'Nothing short of a stunning achievement, a brilliant combination of superb pattern-making and assured draughtsmanship' – or 'the largest postage stamps in the world'? These panels were designed for the House of Lords, but their lordships thought them too gaudy and they have finished up in Swansea civic centre, where the critics are kinder.

Many town halls prefer to retain their original panelling rather than go in for foreign imports, and **Sandwich** Guildhall has kept not only its 1607 panelling but also the jury-box which folds back into it when not in use, rather like a folding bed. It is a feature of the splendidly preserved court room, with its ornamental lamp brackets and fine old paintings. It must be almost a pleasure to be tried there.

Until quite recently **Ilchester** retained in its town hall England's oldest staff of office, a thirteenth-century mace. It still has a mace, but only a replica. The original is on loan to Taunton, but the authorities took note of its inscription, which says in Latin: 'I am a Mark of Amity. Do not forget me (or give me away)'. Hence, no doubt, the presence of the replica.

Sandwich Guildhall (left) has a retractable jury-box which could be folded into the wall like a folding bed (above). Sandwich jurors learned to vacate their seats promptly – or be sandwiched.

Ilchester's thirteenth-century mace is the oldest staff of office in the country (above).

The undignified goings-on at Wokingham town hall (right) in the old days led to the nickname 'lousetown'. The going-on at Marshfield's town or Tolzey hall these days (below) are not very dignified either.

A mark of amity might have come in useful at **Wokingham** town hall in Berkshire when the aldermen were unable to decide who should be mayor. The town hall is in the familiar Victorian mould – a mixture of Gothic, Byzantine and French chateau. But in spite of this grandeur, the argument over the election of the mayor led to Wokingham earning the nickname of 'Lousetown'. It appears that when the aldermen found they could not agree they decided to leave it to a louse. They placed it on the table in their midst and waited for it to make a move. It eventually headed for one of their number, who was forthwith declared elected.

If that seems a little undignified, let me end with a town hall which has achieved even greater ignominy. **Marshfield** in Gloucestershire, once a major malting town famous for its sheep fairs, on the main coach route from London to Bristol, built itself a suitably impressive Town House, or Tolzey, as its civic headquarters. But the maltsters, the sheep, the travellers and indeed the world moved on. The Town House has been converted into public conveniences.

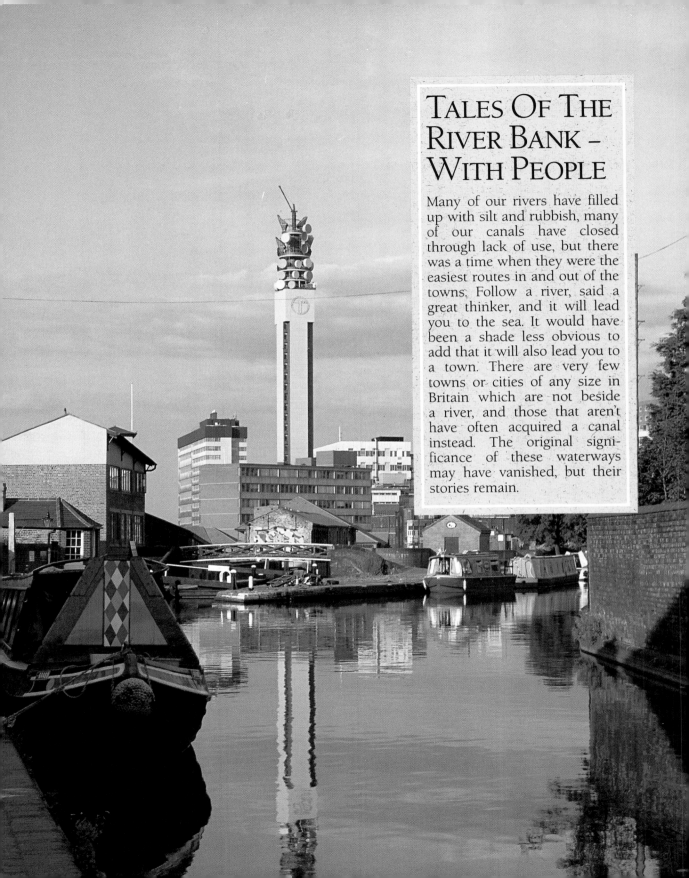

TALES OF THE RIVER BANK – WITH PEOPLE

Many of our rivers have filled up with silt and rubbish, many of our canals have closed through lack of use, but there was a time when they were the easiest routes in and out of the towns. Follow a river, said a great thinker, and it will lead you to the sea. It would have been a shade less obvious to add that it will also lead you to a town. There are very few towns or cities of any size in Britain which are not beside a river, and those that aren't have often acquired a canal instead. The original significance of these waterways may have vanished, but their stories remain.

Once there were 200 Norfolk wherries plying between Norwich and Yarmouth, each able to carry 40 tons of cargo. Now the city's only reminder of these majestic sailing barges is a lonely wherry mast by the River Wensum marking the site of a boat-yard which used to build them.

What better example of a town growing up beside a river – and from my point of view, what example could be more convenient – than **Norwich**, situated where the Rivers Wensum and Yare converge, and the Yare flows on to Great Yarmouth and the sea. Incidentally how convenient also that the geographers decided the Wensum flowed into the Yare, and not the Yare into the Wensum. Great Wensummouth sounds a little unwieldy...

First the Anglo-Saxons settled on the river bank, then the Vikings drove them off, then they returned and got their farms going again – the familiar sequence of village–pillage–tillage. The Normans made Norwich a city, the Dutch weavers made it a port. Steamboats arrived before steam trains, and the Yare became a race-track for competing captains. It came to a head on Good Friday, 1817, when a steam packet called *The Telegraph* raised too much steam and caught a packet. The engine exploded, the boat capsized, half the passengers were killed, and the owner went bankrupt, but his grand-daughter Anna Sewell eventually restored the family fortunes by writing a best seller called *Black Beauty*...

But the most famous craft to use the river was not the steamboat, even an exploding one, but the Norfolk wherry, that majestic sailing barge designed to navigate narrow waterways through flat and wind-swept countryside. Early last century there were 200 of them, each carrying up to 40 tons of cargo. There is still a small jetty near Bishop's Bridge where the city's rubbish was loaded on to wherries to be dumped at sea, and a little upstream there is a reminder of the old sailing barge era, a wherry mast erected on the river bank to mark the site of one of the boat-yards which built them.

Elsewhere in East Anglia the city of **Ely** was served by barges too, and their strangest cargo, so legend has it, was a female corpse. The barge was manned by grave-robbing monks, looking forward to a pat on the pate from the unscrupulous Abbot of Ely.

It is a tale of two Saxon sisters, Withburga and Etheldreda, who both got religion. Etheldreda founded an abbey at

Ely, Withburga founded a nunnery 40 miles away in Norfolk. When food ran short at the nunnery a couple of milch deer answered Withburga's prayers and provided a mobile milk supply. Thus Withburga became a saint and the nunnery became known as **Dereham**, a major centre for pilgrimage and the trade which the pilgrims brought.

Meanwhile, back at the abbey, Etheldreda failed to hit the headlines like her deer-beloved sister and Ely missed out on the pilgrims. Even when the monks built a cathedral and moved into the premier league on the pilgrimage circuit they were still envious of Dereham's star attraction. The abbot sent in the SAS – the Special Abbot Service – to abduct the corpse of St Withburga, which had been safely buried for 300 years.

So it is that on a misty evening in the Fens you may catch a glimpse of a ghostly barge approaching the city, rowed by cowled monks who guard in their midst an open coffin containing Withburga's earthly remains. But the abbot's pernicious ploy failed to achieve its object. Her empty grave filled with water, said to have miraculous properties, and more pilgrims than ever took themselves and

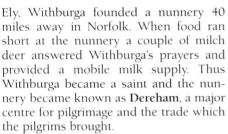

The monks of Ely Cathedral (above) stole the body of St Withburga from Dereham hoping to gain more pilgrims. But the empty grave filled with water, said to have miraculous properties, and St Withburga's Well (left) attracted more pilgrims than ever.

The River Conwy was said to be rich in marvels and mysteries. The estuary was a playground for frolicking mermaids (above), while further upstream (below) St Brigid turned rushes into fishes to end a famine.

their cash to Dereham, to visit St Withburga's Well. While in Ely – well, as you may have noticed, the cathedral is still short of money...

Not every town-and-river tale is quite so gruesome. There is the delightful story of the sparlings of **Conwy** – which I confess I still think of as Conway, and indeed further up the River Conwy on my map there are still the Conway Falls, perhaps to keep English tourists and Welsh locals equally happy. The estuary of the river, where the town stands, was said to be frequented by mermaids, but if you believe all the folklore very few estuaries were mermaid-free, so there is nothing unusual in that. Much more interesting are the little fish which can be caught upstream, called either sparlings or brwyniad, depending whether you favour Conway or Conwy.

These little chaps materialised for the same reason as Withburga's deer, to end a famine. Withburga's opposite number in Conwy, the good St Brigid, tossed some rushes from the river bank into the water, and each rush turned into a fish.

But enough of such charming fancies. Towns mainly relied on their rivers as a means of transport, rather than a source of bedtime stories. The lower reaches of the Thames were once crowded with traffic, and it came under the jurisdiction of the City of London as far upstream as **Staines**. A 'coal post' stands on the river bank in the town as a warning that beyond that point a boat's cargo was subject to the City's taxes. The posts were erected on all the main approaches to London, by road or by water. Most of them date from the late eighteenth century, but some can be found alongside railway lines, which means they were still functioning a hundred years later. Staines also has a much earlier City boundary post, mentioned in the chapter on monuments and memorials.

While the Thames provided the City with taxes, the River Parrett in Somerset provided **Bridgwater** with a much more down-to-earth benefit – or rather, down-to-mud. The Parrett was deep enough for Bridgwater to be a notable port in medieval times but the river silted up, the cloth industry declined, and in the nineteenth century the locals had to look for another source of income. They found it in the river, in the very mud which had ended the town's days as a port. It was baked into oblong chunks and sold as a scourer, to clean grates and steps, under the name of Bath brick.

It was a major local industry from the 1830s onwards and flourished for the best part of a century. But who, I wondered, was the first person to dig up a spadeful of soggy slime and decide to cook it? Did he tell his wife it was a new kind of wholemeal loaf, and watch her break her teeth? Was he trying to invent the breeze-block? Or had he fallen in the river and dried out his clothes in the oven without brushing off the mud? And having baked his mud cake, what prompted him to clean the grate with it?

Such frivolous fancies have been dispelled, alas, by a Mr B. J. Murless, who has wallowed in the history of Bridgwater's mud cakes and come up with a 28-page learned treatise on the subject. The first patent was granted to a local brick maker

in 1818, and other firms along the river soon copied their method of making Bath bricks, Parrett-fashion.

But why not call them Bridgwater bricks? Why name them after a city nearly 40 miles away? Was there a connection with Bath buns, which became popular at about the same time? Or was that first brick maker a Mr Bath?

A 'coal post' by the river at Staines (above) indicated where the City of London made money out of the cargoes. The brick kiln by the river at Bridgwater (below) indicated where the locals made money out of the mud.

The Exeter Ship Canal (right) was built to bypass a weir which made the river impassable (above). Centuries later, the Department of Transport built a motorway bridge which had much the same effect on the canal.

Mr Murless has a mundane answer for that as well. The original patent said the bricks 'would resemble in colour the stone called or known by the name of Bath stone'. So there. But Mr Murless did permit himself a flicker of whimsy amidst the solemn statistics. He quotes from a nineteenth-century ode to the River Parrett: 'Thou flowest ever beautifully thick, Leaving thy filthy slime to make Bath brick.'

While some river towns were losing their trade because of less profitable 'filthy slime', other towns which had no rivers at all were creating their own artificial waterways and calling them ship canals. Manchester is probably the first to come to mind, but the earliest ship canal in England was built down in Devon, to link **Exeter** with the sea. Actually Exeter was already linked by the River Exe, but in the thirteenth century a Countess of Devon with a grudge against the city built a weir so that boats could not sail further upstream than Topsham; from Exeter's point of view the River Exe became an ex-river.

The city fathers brooded on this for 300 years, then leapt into action. They built a canal to bypass the weir, using the first pound locks in Britain. At first it was only 3 feet deep, just enough to take a 16-ton barge, but this was increased to 14 feet over the years, so that a 400-ton cargo ship could sail into the city. Unlike so many canals which were allowed to fall into disuse the Exeter Ship Canal was still being used commercially in the early 1970s. Then after 400 years the story came full circle; instead of a countess building a weir, the Department of Transport built the M5 motorway bridge, the only fixed bridge over the canal and low enough to ensure it will never be used by big ships again.

The West Country had another much longer canal which linked Launceston with the sea at **Bude**, a distance of some 35 miles. The impressive sea lock at Bude still offers a haven for small ships, but the canal itself has been out of action for a century. It was remarkable in that it had no locks apart from that one at the sea end – yet it managed to rise 350 feet. The trick was to use wheeled tub boats at each change of level. They were hooked onto a chain and hauled up a slope to the next section of the canal. Thus Launceston was able to send its grain and slate down to the sea, and sea sand was brought up for fertilisers.

This was the longest canal involving tub boats ever built. It operated for about 70 years, until the railways arrived and provided their own version of tub boats. They strung them together on tracks and called them trains.

Birmingham is one of Britain's very few cities – indeed, one of the few major cities of the world – which was not built alongside a decent-sized river. It has made up for it, however, with canals, a complicated network involving a greater length of waterway than you will find in Venice – though there the resemblance ends. A great deal of it is very hard to find, thanks to the efforts of road and rail engineers, office developers and other space-hungry predators.

Considerable stretches of the canals are out of sight anyway because they were built underground. The canal network known as Birmingham Canal Navigation has the longest and the widest navigable tunnels in Britain, at **Dudley** and **Netherton** respectively. At **Smethwick** a pair of new tunnels take the canal

under a dual carriageway, and at the famous Spaghetti Junction on the M6 motorway there is such an intertwining of concrete above the canal, some of it only a few metres above the water, that it might just as well be another tunnel.

Underneath another stretch of elevated motorway on the M5 you may just be able to spot near the main railway line the three locks at Spon Lane, which are believed to be the oldest working locks in the country. It is a remarkable juxtaposition of three transportation systems, old and new.

Birmingham's network of canals (above) which pass through and under the city are still in commercial use. The canal which reached the sea at Bude sea-lock (below) has been out of action for a century.

Canals deep in the ground and high in the air. The tunnel under Harecastle Hill is 3000 yards long and took 11 years to build (right). The men who built it made their homes by one of the tunnel entrances and founded the town of Kidsgrove. The Pontcysllte Aqueduct (below) 1000 feet long and 120 feet high, is the biggest on any canal in Britain, another triumph for Telford, whose biggest problem was pronouncing it.

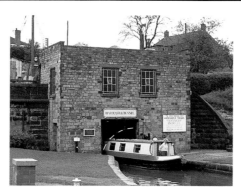

Most canals were built to serve towns which already existed, but in one or two cases it was the canal which created the town. **Kidsgrove**, for instance, came into being largely because of the Trent and Mersey Canal, the dream child of Josiah Wedgwood. Josiah was best known for his pottery but he was also one of the pioneers of canal construction. He got a bill through Parliament for a canal linking the Potteries with the Trent and the Mersey, undeterred by the fact that it would involve a tunnel nearly 3000 yards long through Harecastle Hill.

It took 11 years to dig, and the men who worked on it set up home at one of the entrances and became the first residents of Kidsgrove. The tunnel was opened in 1777, to the amazement of local sceptics. They had a chance to jeer again less than 50 years later, when the hill started subsiding on it, but Thomas Telford, who dug tunnels with less effort than most of us dig the garden, promptly created another one alongside the first.

The twin entrances on each side of Harecastle Hill are still an impressive sight; the original tunnel is out of action but Telford's has been restored and is back in use.

Canals do not exactly find a welcome in the Welsh hillsides; it is tricky terrain for anything that has to stay level for any distance. As a result those that did get built are very spectacular, and the **Llangollen** Canal claims to be the prettiest narrow canal in Britain, centred on one of Wales's prettiest towns. Pontcysllte Aqueduct, over 1000 feet long and 120 feet high, is the biggest on any canal. The iron trough which carries the water has dovetailed iron joints to prevent it leaking, and the 'towpath' was built above it to allow the canal itself to be the full width of the aqueduct. Pontcysllte was another Telford triumph; his biggest problem, I imagine, was pronouncing it.

Finally, the waterways that were dug not for transport but for drainage. Without these dykes much of Cambridgeshire, Lincolnshire and West Norfolk would still be just a soggy mess. It all started, not with the Dutch engineers of the seventeenth century who finally drained the Fens, but with the Romans. **Bourne** in Lincolnshire is mainly famous as the birthplace of Hereward the Wake, and, rather later, as the home of BRM racing cars, but it also has the Roman Car Dyke, the earliest attempt to drain the land sufficiently for people to live there. Happily it was successful, and Bourne was born.

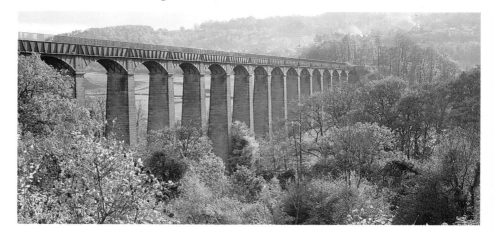

CASTLES NOT ENTIRELY IN THE AIR

Castles in the air, like pipe dreams and pie in the sky, are not expected to become reality – but the chap who coined the phrase thought they should. 'If you have built castles in the air', said Thoreau, 'your work need not be lost; that is where it should be. Now put the foundations under them.' Perhaps that is how some of the ancient castles in England and Wales took shape – a wild idea converted amazingly and often expensively into bricks and mortar. As a result even the most forbidding of them may have some entertaining features, some unusual stories, and some very odd imitations.

Caernarvon Castle was built with octagonal towers and bands of different coloured masonry, in the Turkish style. It is said that this was Edward I's idea, because he believed the Emperor Constantine, founder of Constantinople, was born at Caernarvon. Or did the master mason just have a fancy for brown and white stripes?

Edward I, as every schoolboy used to know, was called the Hammer of the Scots, and he did knock them about pretty thoroughly. But when it came to the Welsh he switched from hammering to hamming, and made a very theatrical appearance on the battlements of **Caernarvon** Castle holding aloft his new-born son, to proclaim him Prince of Wales.

The Welsh were not terribly impressed. Nor indeed was his infant son, who caught a chill as a result which nearly ended his princely career as soon as it began. It was another couple of centuries before Wales and England got together under Henry Tudor, who as it happened was also born in a Welsh castle, at Pembroke, but fortunately for his health did not have such a histrionic father.

Edward soon gave up brandishing babies and concentrated on castles instead. He put up nine of them in North Wales, most of which are still standing, entirely or in part. If you visit them, spare a thought not only for the king who commissioned them but the remarkable chap who actually built them, a mason from Savoy called Master James of St George.

Master James was still working on Caernarvon when Edward did his turn with Edward Junior on the battlements. The king aimed to make it the seat of government for the principality, the Windsor of Wales, and his mason left no stone unturned – indeed he must have used every stone he could lay his hands on – to achieve that aim. But it doesn't look much like Windsor; on the contrary, it looks far more like Constantinople.

Unlike any other Welsh castle of that period, the towers are octagonal instead of square or circular, and the walls have bands of different coloured masonry, brown sandstone alternating with lighter-coloured limestone. The story goes that Edward ordered his mason to copy this Turkish style because he believed the Emperor Constantine, founder of Constantinople, was born at Caernarvon. But I wonder if Master James just had a fancy for brown and white stripes?

While King Edward was erecting his chain of state-owned castles in North Wales, private enterprise was hard at it in the south. His son-in-law Gilbert de Clare – who must have enjoyed issuing proclamations which started, 'I, de Clare, declare . . .' – was going it alone at **Caerphilly**. He built a castle with a fortified barrage, an amazing medieval dam nearly 400 yards long which created a 12-foot deep lake around the castle. This super moat was designed to keep out of range the siege catapults used to breach castle walls. The dam had to be protected of course, or the catapults could have breached that instead, so it had towers and defensive platforms. The thickness and strength of the dam was quite remarkable; today's hydraulic engineers with all their modern equipment and technology could hardly have done better.

Yet in spite of all these precautions, that dedicated demolition expert Oliver Cromwell managed to knock Caerphilly about a bit, along with every other castle he came across. He left behind him a tower which leans at an even steeper

Caerphilly Castle had a remarkable defence system, a fortified barrage which created a lake around the castle. But Cromwell still managed to knock it about a bit, as its tilting tower bears witness.

Pembroke Castle has a distinction shared by BBC Television, a Wogan – but in this case it is a huge cavern under the castle. It was probably named after the Earl's agent at the time.

angle than the Tower of Pisa. No doubt he thought that wind and weather would finish the job for him, but it leans there still.

It was an earlier Gilbert de Clare who became the first Earl of Pembroke in 1138 and master of **Pembroke** Castle, which had the distinction among Welsh castles of never being taken, even briefly, by the Welsh. It also has the distinction, shared only by BBC Television, of having a Wogan – which perhaps is why the Welsh didn't try to capture it.

The Pembroke Wogan, however, is not a talkative invader from across the Irish Sea but a huge cavern cut out of the limestone under the castle and reached by a spiral staircase, partly cut out of the rock. The cavern opens on to the river and could have been ideal as an emergency exit or for bringing in a spot of contraband. Actually its purpose was probably more mundane; it was just used as a boat-house.

But why Wogan? Could this be an ancient Celtic word describing something of unusual character, with considerable potential which is rarely put to full use? Nothing so subtle. The Earl of Pembroke had an agent in 1291 called John Wogan and it was probably named after him.

Cardiff Castle has some unexpected features too, but of more recent origin. The third Marquis of Bute inherited the title when he was 6 months old and when he became 18 in 1865 decided to remodel the castle, which his family owned along with most of Cardiff. He created some very strange, almost surrealistic rooms within the ancient walls, from the smoking room with astrological decorations in the clock tower to the Arab room with stalactites painted with gold leaf. Smoking and stars? Arabs and stalactites? Don't ask me, ask the Marquis – who was keen on spiritualism, and might actually reply.

Back in the days when castles were for fighting, not for fun, the English not only built them in Wales to keep the Welsh down, but along the English border, to keep them out. The most notable one that remains is at **Ludlow**, a town which was created at the same time as the castle. 'They were united', said one writer, 'in indissoluble marriage.' Another waxed more ecstatic: 'The castle is probably without rival in Britain for the sylvan beauty of its position, in which wood and water, and meadows of wide expanse and rare fertility, are combined with rugged and lofty crags.' It was also a jolly good position for killing Welshmen, and it was used successfully for this purpose for 200 years.

The original castle was wooden, but in 1140 the first stone addition was erected, and it remains one of the most unusual features of any of our castles, because it is a chapel with a circular nave. Only about half a dozen churches in Britain have this kind of nave – the Temple Church in London is probably the best known; the Romanesque church of Orphir in the Orkneys is probably the most obscure. Ludlow is the only castle I know of with a chapel like this, modelled on the Church of the Holy Sepulchre in Jerusalem.

The ancient chapel of Ludlow Castle has a circular nave, one of the few in Britain and the only one inside a castle. Like the Temple Church in London, it is modelled on the Church of the Holy Sepulchre in Jerusalem.

The prison chapel in Lincoln Castle has the ultimate in box pews. No prisoner was allowed any contact with his neighbour (right). Robin Hood had no such problems contacting Maid Marian or his Merry Men at Nottingham Castle (below).

was deprived of a beer allowance for three days, for the second he lost it for a week. Presumably the large roller-skate on which the beer travelled up and down the servants' table would sail straight past him. If there was a third misdemeanour, then a very nasty moment indeed: 'his offence would be laid before the Master'.

The penalties inflicted at **Lincoln** Castle were far more drastic than missing out on the beer barrel. Like Norwich and many other castles, Lincoln was used for many years as a prison, and the tower known as Cobb Hall was designed for the purpose, with rings in the walls to chain up the prisoners and a gallows on the roof to hang them. The castle chapel is a far cry from the splendour of St George's, Windsor; it has a partition between each seat so the prisoners could not see each other during the service – the box pew principle taken to extremes.

Nottingham Castle inevitably has reminders of Robin Hood. The medieval castle is in ruins but Robin survives. There is a statue of him in what looks like a winged helmet at first glance; it is actually a hat with a feather in it. The statue is cleanshaven, but there are three reliefs on the wall which can't

An eagle is said to have dropped the arm of St Oswald on the site of Oswestry Castle – and thus gave the castle and the town its name.

decide whether he used a razor or not; he has a beard in two of them and none in the third. As I recall, filmstar Errol Flynn favoured the bearded version while Richard Greene was never without his Gillette . . .

Little is left of **Oswestry** Castle; it was given the full treatment by Cromwell's gunpowder experts. What they could not destroy, however, was King Oswald's Well, which is still a feature of the public park where the castle once stood. Legend has it that after King Oswald, the Christian king of Northumbria, was slain by the pagan Penda in 642, an eagle seized his arm – presumably severed in the fighting – and flew off with it to Oswestry, where he dropped it on the spot where the well is now. Thus Oswald gave his arm as well as his name to Oswestry. This slightly extravagant tale is recorded on an official plaque, which also bears the much more mundane information that 'A scheme of improvements to the well and surrounds was undertaken by Oswestry Town Council in 1985'.

While Oswestry Castle has been reduced to fragments of wall, the Roman fortifications at **Lincoln** have been reduced to a gateway, known confusingly as the Newport Arch. The Romans built it just wide enough to take a column of soldiers or a medium-size chariot. Today it can accommodate a car and a pedestrian; it is the only Roman gateway in Britain still used by traffic.

The Romans designed the Newport Arch in Lincoln to take a column of soldiers or a medium-sized chariot. Today it is the only Roman gateway in Britain still used by traffic.

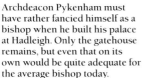

Archdeacon Pykenham must have rather fancied himself as a bishop when he built his palace at Hadleigh. Only the gatehouse remains, but even that on its own would be quite adequate for the average bishop today.

The Deanery Tower at **Hadleigh** in Suffolk is all that remains of a grandiose palace which was built, not for an archbishop or even a bishop, but for Archdeacon Pykenham, a fifteenth-century cleric with ideas above his station. Judging by the magnificence of the gatehouse, with its towers and turrets, the actual palace must have been very grand indeed.

There is a much more modest gatehouse, with less spectacular turrets, at **Tavistock** in Devon. The Fitzford Gate was the entrance to a private house which no longer exists, and I only include it because of the macabre tale attached to it. On certain nights of the year, it is said, a coach made of bones and drawn by

headless horses comes thundering through the gate, carrying the ghost of a beautiful woman. Preceding it runs a black hound with one eye in the middle of its forehead. This gruesome cortège stops at Okehampton church, where the woman plucks a blade of grass in the churchyard, regards it gloomily, then cries the spectral equivalent of 'Home James!' and they all go back to Fitzford Gate.

This is Lady Howard, doing penance for the murder of her four husbands, two of whom she disposed of before she was 16. A chronicler with a boring eye for accuracy has pointed out that at best this story can be only 75 per cent true, since Lady Howard's fourth husband managed to survive her. But when you are offered a beautiful ghost in a bony coach, a team of headless horses and a one-eyed dog, who's bothering to count the corpses?

Now some 'castles' that aren't. If you enter **Morpeth** in Northumberland by the main road from the south you will be faced by a massive battlemented tower which looks as if it has seen many a fierce skirmish with marauding Scots. Actually it was the court-house and police station, and is now a restaurant with apartments. All that is left of the real Morpeth Castle is a restored gatehouse elsewhere in the town, and even that is being converted into flats.

Far away from Northumberland, on the south coast of Wales, there stands on a hill above **Swansea** the gaunt remains of Morris Castle, tall stone ruins which were never a castle but an eighteenth-century

The Fitzford Gate (right), scene of a spectral coach-ride, with a skeleton driver, headless horses and a one-eyed dog.

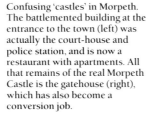

Confusing 'castles' in Morpeth. The battlemented building at the entrance to the town (left) was actually the court-house and police station, and is now a restaurant with apartments. All that remains of the real Morpeth Castle is the gatehouse (right), which has also become a conversion job.

The bleak ruins of Morriston Castle (above) were actually a block of flats, perhaps the earliest tower block in Britain, built to avoid the fumes in the valley. Bude Castle (below) was built on a concrete raft to avoid sinking in the sand, the nearest we can get to a 'castle in the air'.

Sir John decided to house his employees on the hillside above the valley, away from the fumes of the mills. Morris Castle was built to house forty families with premises for a shoemaker and a tailor. He also built the model village of Morriston with a church in the centre. The original houses have been replaced and Morris Castle is in ruins, but the name of Sir John Morris has been retained, a tribute to an employer ahead of his time.

Incidentally the 'castle' which was never a castle is now near neighbour to a 'cathedral' which was never a cathedral. The Capel Tabernacle, large enough to seat nearly 2000 people and the home of the Morriston Orpheus Choir, is popularly referred to as the Cathedral of Welsh Nonconformity.

Finally there is **Bude** Castle, which is its correct name although it has no towers or turrets, and stands only two storeys high. These days it serves the unromantic role of council offices, but its story has a touch of romance none the less. An ingenious eighteenth-century engineer called Sir Goldsworthy Gurney decided to challenge the Biblical warning about building on sand. He erected his castle on a raft of concrete which he 'floated' on the sand at Summerlease Beach.

That was about 160 years ago, and Bude Castle hasn't sunk yet. Perhaps it is the nearest we shall get to building a 'castle in the air' . . .

block of flats, perhaps the earliest tower block in Britain. It was built by a kindly copper master called Sir John Morris, who inherited a vast empire of copper works, collieries and brass-wire mills in and around Landore. At that time the Lower Swansea Valley looked a fair imitation of Hell, with the fumes and green flames rising from the furnaces. A popular local rhyme summed it up:

> *It came to pass in days of yore,*
> *the Devil chanced upon Landore.*
> *Quoth he, 'By all this fume and stink,*
> *I can't be far from home, I think.'*

MARKETS, EXCHANGES – AND COUNTER ATTRACTIONS

First there were the informal markets, either on the square around the market cross or under cover in a market hall, where countryfolk brought their produce. Then they started making things as well as growing things, and it occurred to them how convenient it would be to cut out the commuting and have permanent premises in town. So they put up buildings around the markets with living quarters upstairs, a workshop out the back, and a front room with hinged shutters opening on to the street. The lower shutter folded downwards to form a table, the other opened upwards to provide cover. They had invented 'the shop'.

Alston's market cross has been demolished twice in the last 20 years by errant lorries failing to negotiate the cobbles on the steep hill. Now the bollards should protect it – at least, that's what those three tourists seem to think . . .

Every market town had its market cross as the focal point for its commercial activities, and if civic leaders have had any sensitivity at all they have managed to preserve them in their original positions. It has not always been easy – and not just because of the depredations of developers. **Alston** in Cumbria, for instance, has a particular problem with traffic.

Alston is one of the highest market towns in the country, built on a very steep hill. The main street would be tricky enough for heavy vehicles to negotiate in any case, but cobble-stones are still used to surface it and these can be very treacherous in wet weather. The market cross stood beside the road for centuries without suffering any great harm; the odd encounter with a horse wagon or a stage-coach would only have dented it. But once the 38-tonners started trundling through the town it came under constant threat.

A runaway lorry knocked it down in 1971. They rebuilt it, and it was knocked down again in 1980; so they rebuilt it

again. When I was last in Alston the cross looked in good shape, but if these things happen in 9-year cycles, as I write this another lorry is just about due . . .

The market cross at **Barnard Castle** in County Durham was struck for quite a different reason, and it still bears the scars. It happened because of an argument between a soldier and a gamekeeper in 1804. Each claimed to be the better shot. They stood outside the Turk's Head inn, where their argument had probably developed, and each took a pot at the weather-vane on the market cross, a hundred yards away. Amazingly each of them hit it. They declared a draw and doubtless returned to the bar. The bullet holes in the weather-vane are still there.

The market cross beneath the weathervane is a very solid and serviceable structure, an octagonal stone building on pillars where the butter market was held at ground level and the upper room was used as a lock-up and later as a court room. Many of these structures, however, were built as much for decoration as occupation, such as the ornate fifteenth-century Poultry Cross in **Salisbury**, which stands almost menacingly on its great stone legs like some medieval spaceship. In complete contrast there is the butter cross at **Swaffham** in Norfolk, which is not a cross at all but a domed rotunda which the Earl of Orford erected in 1783. The lady on top has been variously described as the Goddess of Plenty, or the Goddess of Agriculture, or both. No Earl of Orford survives today to say precisely what his forebear had in mind.

The sturdy market cross at Barnard Castle (above) still has two bullet-holes in its weathervane, the result of a shooting match nearly 200 years ago between two customers of the Turk's Head (far left). Salisbury's more elaborate Poultry Cross (left) has so far remained unscathed.

While country markets offered poultry and butter and other farm produce, seaside towns offered fish. The fish merchants often had permanent sites on the market, with stone or slate tables where they laid out their catch and fixed a price. Curiously these were frequently close to the stocks, where other strange fish were displayed for inspection. Perhaps part of their punishment was to be tantalised by the fishy odours; they might also provide handy targets for unwanted fish heads.

Fish and whips at Poulton-le-Fylde (above, right), but the fishmongers and miscreants have long since gone; certainly the stocks (right) could no longer hold them. But the fish slabs and stocks at Broughton-in-Furness (top and above) still look quite serviceable.

Broughton-in-Furness in Cumbria is a good example of this juxtaposition. In the square under the chestnut trees the stocks beside the fish table are still in working order. Poulton-le-Fylde in Lancashire has a similar arrangement, with a whipping post as a bonus, but the holes in the stocks have long since merged into one.

A different kind of table existed in some towns for merchants to strike their bargains. In Queen Anne's Walk in Barnstaple, an eighteenth-century colonnade with a splendid statue of Queen Anne perched on top, the merchants' money table, known as the Tome Stone, still stands in its niche. And outside the Exchange in **Bristol** are four bronze pillars, looking rather like bird-tables, which were known as the 'nails' on which merchants put down their money. Thus was derived the saying, 'pay on the nail', which sounds a lot more authoritative than 'pay on the bird-table'.

Understandably the merchants liked to trade under cover if they could, which led to the development of exchanges like Bristol's. Most of them were corn exchanges; there are examples in a great many of our market towns, some more elegant than others. **Rochester**'s has been embellished with an enormous clock overhanging the street, while **Hitchin** in Hertfordshire has an Italianate Corn Exchange built by the Victorians with a Venetian window and a lantern turret.

They 'paid on the nail' in Bristol (above) and on the Tome Stone in Barnstaple (left and below).

Victorian Corn Exchanges were not just places of business, they were architectural works of art – if you like that sort of thing. Hitchin favoured the Italian style, with Venetian windows and a lantern turret (right).

Two extremes in agricultural markets: the elaborate Corn Exchange in King's Lynn with a goddess presiding on the roof (above), and what is left of the Old Shambles at Shepton Mallet, more like a bus shelter than a meat market (above, right).

Many of them, like the Corn Exchange in **King's Lynn**, have a statue on top of Ceres, Goddess of Agriculture – or is it the Goddess of Plenty? **Dereham**, 30 miles away, decided to vary the pattern and invested in a statue of Norfolk's agricultural hero, Coke of Norfolk, but the Goddess of Agriculture (or Plenty?) was obviously furious at being slighted and knocked him off the Corn Exchange roof in the 1950s with a bolt of lightning. The building itself, like so many redundant Corn Exchanges, has been given over to films and bingo.

Not every exchange dealt in corn. In earlier days there were meat markets, known as Shambles, and **Shepton Mallet** in Somerset is one of the towns where a vestige of the Old Shambles remains, in the form of a fifteenth-century wooden shed. Unfortunately it looks more like a bus shelter than a meat market, with a large seat under a tiled roof, but this was for butchers, not bus passengers.

The Shambles at **Stroud** in Gloucestershire still exists, though it is now known as the Town Hall and the only marketing that takes place there is carried out by the Women's Institute. It has been much altered and restored since the sixteenth century, but there are still two columns in the centre with stone brackets. The story goes that the columns were originally adorned by two gargoyle-like faces, the inspiration of the churchwardens, a Mr

Chambers and a Mr Barter. The town promptly christened the gargoyles Chambers and Barter, which so discomfited these solemn gentlemen that they removed the heads and put plain blocks of stone instead. Their names live on, however, since the Council uses Chambers on the upper floor, and the WI, I am sure, have not forgotten how to Barter.

Specialised exchanges were built in towns with particular products. The wool merchants of **Halifax** had the Piece Hall,

'piece' referring to the pieces of cloth which were sold there by the weavers. They set out their wares in 300 little rooms which opened off the colonnaded galleries around the central quadrangle – sometimes on two levels, sometimes on three, since the hall was built on a slope. Piece Hall is the only cloth hall to survive in Yorkshire, but instead of weavers the rooms are now occupied, inevitably, by craft shops, antiques, books and a tourist office.

Piece Hall in Halifax, the only surviving cloth hall in Yorkshire, though its rooms are now occupied by craft shops and antique dealers instead of weavers; but the fleece still remains on the weathervane.

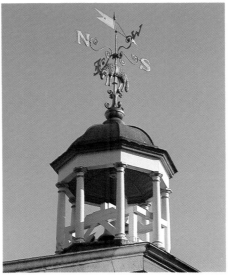

The town hall at Stroud (above) still has the columns which embarrassed the churchwardens in its days as a Shambles.

Whitstable and Witney each built special centres for their most famous local products. Whitstable has the Royal Native Oyster Stores (top, right), and Witney has the Blanket Hall (above), with its one-handed clock. But Witney produced butter too, and its butter cross goes one better than the Blanket Hall – its clock has two hands (top).

Whitstable in Kent has a building which is not strictly an exchange but certainly looks grand enough to be one, and like Witney's Blanket Hall and Halifax's Piece Hall it specialises in the town's most famous local product. The Royal Native Oyster Stores were erected to cope with the products of Whitstable's oyster hatchery, the largest in Europe, and it comes into its own each July during the Oyster Festival. Inside it displays the coats of arms which indicate that Queen Victoria and her grandson George V both bought their oysters here.

Alongside the big exchanges where the early wholesalers did business, individual retailers were opening up their own premises to sell direct to the public.

The oldest commercial bakery in Britain is claimed to be Jacka's Bakery in Southside Street, **Plymouth**. It is reputed to be where the ship's biscuits were made for the *Mayflower* – but perhaps that should be taken with a pinch of flour. **Knaresborough** in North Yorkshire, not to be outdone, claims to have Britain's oldest chemist's shop, but this is a little difficult to prove, since potions have been purchased by the public since the days when the main retail outlets were witches' caves. And there is a manufacturing chemist in **Hitchin** who pursues his business in a fourteenth-century gatehouse. Could he argue that his establishment is

Witney in Oxfordshire had a specialist market also; being Witney, it is of course the Blanket Hall. It was built in 1720 and is an unexceptional building except for the balls perched on each front corner, and an unusual one-handed clock from which you can work out the time to the nearest quarter-hour. Unexpectedly Witney also has a butter cross; one gets so attuned to Witney blankets one forgets there might be Witney butter too. That also has a clock, with a sundial for good measure. Whether you sought blankets or butter, they liked you to be punctual in Witney.

older than Knaresborough's? Perhaps Knaresborough is safer with its other claim to commercial antiquity; it has England's oldest linen mill.

Southam in Warwickshire does have an indisputable place in the history of dispensing chemists. The first Provident Dispensary was established there in 1823, to supply medicines and medical advice to the poor. The idea caught on and was copied in Coventry, Northampton and elsewhere. The dispensary itself, alas, no longer exists; just a small monument marks where it stood. Incidentally it was here that garden allotments were established 'for the early instruction of boys in the management of land' – another innovative development. A plaque records proudly that the Speaker of the House of Commons, no less, dropped by to see how the boys were getting on.

Jacka's Bakery in Plymouth (above) not only dates back to Victorian days (above, left); it is said to have supplied ship's biscuits to the Mayflower.

Knaresborough claims to have the oldest chemist's shop in Britain (below, left); Britain's oldest Provident Dispensary is now only marked by a monument at Southam (below).

Two examples of business enterprise: the sign of a TV dealer trying to create a period atmosphere at Llantrisant (above), and the sign of a clockmaker who did a useful deal with the council at Guildford (below).

It was not always easy for a craftsman or a professional man to set up shop in a town. John Aylward ran into problems when he tried to open a clock-making business in **Guildford** in 1683. The city fathers objected and refused permission. Mr Aylward then adopted a form of persuasion which has been widely followed by developers today to influence a council's decision. Let me start my business, he said, and I will give you a splendid new clock for your Guildhall. The city fathers accepted his generous gesture – surely not a bribe? – and Mr Aylward got

his shop. The clock is still there on the Guildhall; surprisingly, its face is not red.

Many shopkeepers find it is good business to preserve the venerable atmosphere of their premises. Some even try to invent it; at **Llantrisant**, for example, there is actually 'Ye Olde Television Shoppe'. But most are quite genuine. **Wolverhampton** has a tea merchant's shop in Queen Street which has hardly changed in appearance for a century and a half; the old brass scales are still on the mahogany counter, the tea canisters emblazoned with the flags of their country of origin are still on the shelves behind. Perhaps in deference to changing tastes, the window now displays rather more coffee than tea.

One of the most famous old retail establishments is the shop of the Tailor of **Gloucester**. You will be familiar with Beatrix Potter's version of the story – how the tailor fell ill while he was making a wedding suit for the mayor, and the mice worked through the night to finish it on time, all but one buttonhole on which they left the message, 'No more twist'. But here's the story behind the story.

There really was a tailor of Gloucester, who really did fall ill while making a waistcoat for the mayor – not to be married in, but for the opening of the annual flower show. The tailor left the unfinished waistcoat in the shop on Saturday evening. When he returned on Monday morning it had been completed, except for one buttonhole which bore the message, 'No more twist'. The enterprising tailor forthwith put a notice in the window announcing that if you ordered a suit from him the fairies would finish it overnight.

What actually happened was that his assistants had fallen asleep in the shop after spending Saturday night in the pubs. They did not like to emerge on the Sunday, unshaven and dishevelled, while church-goers were passing the shop on their way to and from the cathedral. So they waited until nightfall, and to pass the time they worked on the waistcoat – until they ran out of twist at the last buttonhole. No doubt the tailor, and in due course Miss Potter, decided not to let the

facts spoil a good story, so the notice stayed in the window and the Tailor of Gloucester became known throughout the world.

Even the shop itself is a mixture of fact and fancy. Miss Potter copied its exterior in her book, but her drawings of the interior were based on a local cottage which she had visited. When her enterprising publishers later acquired the shop they remodelled the interior to look like her drawings. It now offers for sale, not fairy-finished finery but popular Potter pottery.

An old shop at **Rochdale** in Lancashire marks a real-life milestone in the history of the retail trade. This was where the Co-op was born. In 1844, when the flannel weavers in the town were suffering the

The tea merchant of Wolverhampton, W. T. M. Snape, where the interior has hardly changed for 150 years (left and below, left); and the Tailor of Gloucester, now transformed into a Beatrix Potter memento shop (below).

effects of a long and unsuccessful strike, they each contributed a sovereign to open a shop in Toad Lane run on co-operative principles; the customers shared all the profits. The Rochdale Equitable Pioneers' Society prospered and expanded; there is now even a Chateau Rochdale wine, named by a wine-growing co-operative in Southern France in honour of the Rochdale pioneers.

The original shop in Toad Lane – the name comes, not from a toad, but from the Lancashire pronunciation of 't'owd lane' – is now a museum, but the whole of one outside wall is still emblazoned with its original advertisement, 'Delicious Co-op Tea'.

The earliest specialist banks outside London were opened in the 1770s. Not many of the original buildings are still used for the same purpose, but one exception is the former Black Ox Bank in **Llandovery**, Dyfed, which was founded by a drover called David Jones to serve the cattle owners who frequented the town. After the death of Jones the Bank, it continued to function until 1909, when it was bought by Lloyds Bank and the Black Ox was replaced by the Black Horse.

Finally a petrol station which is well on the way to becoming an antique. **Stockbridge** in Hampshire was a posting station on the Roman road from Winchester to Salisbury, and one still finds occasional traces of their passing. Then came the Welsh drovers, perhaps all the way from Llandovery, taking their cattle to the wealthy markets in the Home Counties; they left behind some Welsh inscriptions on a former pub near the river.

With the coming of the motor car it became the main route for holiday-makers heading for the West Country, until the motorways were built and the traffic left Stockbridge in comparative peace. It also left this petrol station, which still has the old-fashioned arms on the pumps so they can swing out above the pavement to reach the cars on the road. The building has an old balcony with iron railings and the roof looks like a Victorian railway station.

It would be nice to think that the pumps still showed the cost of a gallon in shillings and pence, but even this splendid old survivor of motoring in the thirties has had to succumb to the new money – and worse still, to that foreign invader, the litre . . .

Survivors of earlier trading styles: the shop in Rochdale where the Co-op was born (right), which is honoured even in the French vineyards (above), and a period-piece petrol station in Stockbridge (below) which now has to honour French litres.

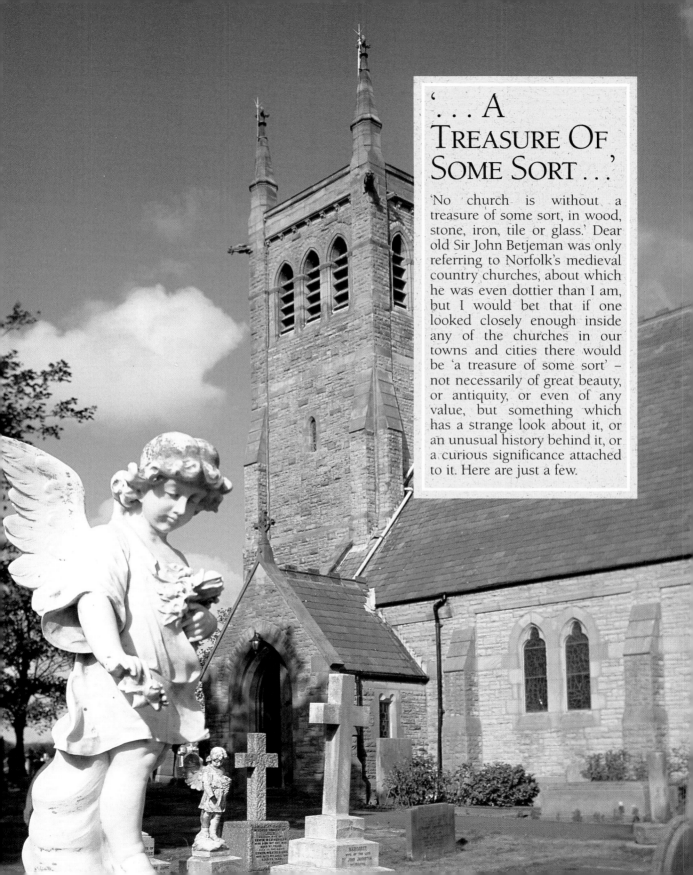

'... A TREASURE OF SOME SORT ...'

'No church is without a treasure of some sort, in wood, stone, iron, tile or glass.' Dear old Sir John Betjeman was only referring to Norfolk's medieval country churches, about which he was even dottier than I am, but I would bet that if one looked closely enough inside any of the churches in our towns and cities there would be 'a treasure of some sort' – not necessarily of great beauty, or antiquity, or even of any value, but something which has a strange look about it, or an unusual history behind it, or a curious significance attached to it. Here are just a few.

Sometimes it is the church itself which qualifies as a sort of treasure because of its design, or its position, or its history. The Welsh would doubtless point to the fourteenth-century church of St Giles at **Wrexham**, the tower of which has been called one of the Seven Wonders of Wales. Certainly it is one of the highest, one of the most pinnacled and one of the most ornamented; but it is also one of the most obvious. I prefer to admire **Tewkesbury** Abbey, not just because it is a fine-looking abbey church but because of the devotion of past parishioners of Tewkesbury in keeping it that way.

I don't mean the struggle which every parish has to preserve the fabric of its church. In Tewkesbury's case the towns-people were so determined to save the abbey from desecration and probably destruction during the dissolution of the monasteries that they raised enough money to buy the building from Henry VIII, lock, stock and pulpit. Thus they

were able to preserve the splendid Norman tower and nave, and the six-fold arch in the west front, the largest of its kind in Britain.

Glastonbury Abbey was not so fortunate. Unimpressed by the legend that King Arthur and Queen Guinevere were buried there, Henry's demolition experts did a thorough job on the abbey. Fortunately, however, they left one of its more unusual buildings intact. It is the Abbot's Kitchen, where his meals were prepared over the open fires in each corner of the room. The four chimneys converged on the central stone lantern on the roof, which might have been mistaken for a look-out tower were it not for the smoke coming out of its windows. The kitchen is now used as a museum to show the kind of meal the Abbot enjoyed; it was very different from the frugal fare supplied by the monks' kitchen, which perhaps the monks were quite glad to see pulled down . . .

Tewkesbury Abbey was preserved for posterity by the devotion of the townspeople. To save it from desecration and probably destruction during the dissolution of the monasteries they raised enough money to buy it from Henry VIII – lock, stock and pulpit.

The Abbot's Kitchen at Glastonbury with its central 'lantern', actually a chimney (above and above, right).

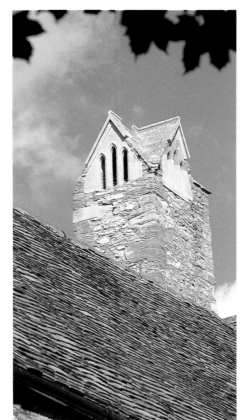

Abingdon Abbey also had its distinctive chimney (left), not over the kitchen but the Checker, or Exchequer; if any cooking was done, it was only the books.

Abingdon Abbey in Oxfordshire also suffered at Henry's hands, but here too there remains a curious chimney on top of a square stone building which escaped his attentions. It was not the kitchen but the Checker, or Exchequer, where if anything was cooked it was only the books. Nevertheless its thirteenth-century builders provided it with this striking chimney; the smoke emerges from the holes beneath the little gabled roof.

In more recent times the church of St Mary's in **Guildford** faced a threat from another king, though not of such a drastic nature. The central apse of the church

St Mary's church in Guildford used to project further out into the road, but George IV ordered part of it to be removed so that his coach had a clear run through the town.

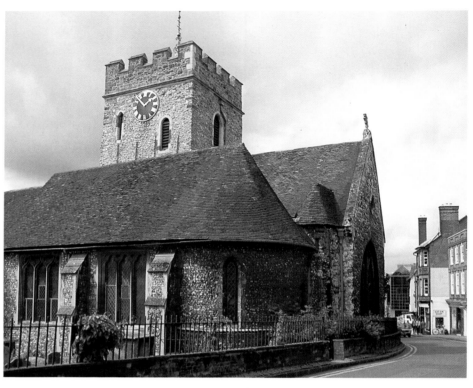

It looks as though there was a similar problem at Walsall, but rather than chop back St Matthew's church they put the road underneath it. But there is a more likely explanation.

faces on to Quarry Street, and until 1825 it used to stick out rather further than it does today. Apparently George IV became irritated when his coachman had to slow down to drive round it. He ordered that the curved end of the apse should be removed and the rest of it shortened. The parishioners may have been left a little cramped but the royal coach was given a clear run.

There was a similar clash of interests between church and state, so it is said, when road engineers at **Walsall** in the West Midlands found that St Matthew's church lay in the path of their proposed main road to Birmingham. In this case, however, they found a happier compromise, by constructing the vaulted tunnel which runs underneath the church, and routing the road through that. A more likely explanation for the tunnel and the walkway that leads into it is that they were constructed when the church was extended to the edge of the churchyard, so that processions could still walk right round it without going into the road.

Church treasures rediscovered. Priests' robes from pre-Reformation days were discovered in the sealed-up crypt of St Elphin's church, Warrington, and returned to the Roman Catholics.

In the year before Guildford lost a part of its church which had stood for centuries, **Warrington** found a part of its church which had been lost for centuries. The crypt of St Elphin's church was sealed up in Elizabeth I's reign and only rediscovered in 1824. On the steps leading down to it were found a medieval chalice and the robes of two priests, dating from pre-Reformation days. Presumably the Catholics put them there in something of a hurry before sealing the crypt, to hide them from the Protestants. The Rector who found them generously handed them back to the Roman Catholic church of St Alban's in Bewsey Street, where they still remain.

The Catholics of **Shifnal** in Shropshire have also had an ancient relic restored to them. Their golden chalice disappeared after the Reformation, but some security-conscious monk, fearing either that it would be stolen or, like a hotel key, be inadvertently removed by a visitor, engraved upon it the polite request:

Return mee to Sheafnall in Shropshire.

The golden chalice of Shifnal was rediscovered in a York antiques shop after 400 years and the purchaser obeyed its inscription: *'Return mee to Sheafnall in Shropshire'*.

The sanctuary seat at Beverley Minster, also known as the Frith Stool. Fugitives who gave all their money to the church and promised to serve it were allowed to stay in Beverley as Frithmen. Americans might regard this as citing the Frith Amendment . . .

For 400 years the request was ignored, then the chalice turned up in an antiques shop in Yorkshire and its honest purchaser duly returned it to 'Sheafnall'.

The Augustinian priory at **Dunstable** in Bedfordshire was dissolved along with all the others at the Reformation, but one of its treasures must have escaped the marauders because St Peter's church, originally part of the priory, still has the Fayrey Pall, presented by a rich local merchant called Henry Fayrey for use as a coffin covering at family funerals. It depicts St John the Baptist in a rough coat of camel's hair, with Mr Fayrey leading a group of men towards him on one side, and Mrs Fayrey heading a group of ladies on the other – all of them considerably better-clad than St John. It was no doubt used for Henry Fayrey's own coffin in 1516.

In the days before Henry VIII raided the monasteries, Oliver Cromwell wrecked the churches and George IV lopped the ends off apses, such places were able to offer sanctuary, not only to precious possessions but to people. The priory church of St Margaret with St Mary Magdalene and all the Virgin Saints – St

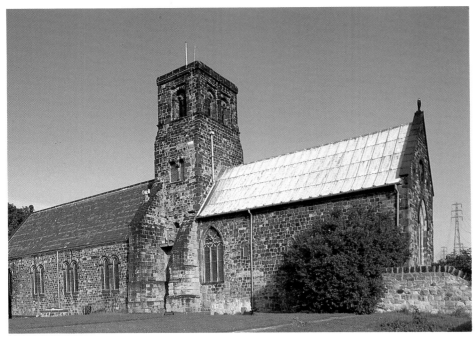

St Paul's Church in Jarrow, and the wooden chair which is said to have been used by the Venerable Bede when he wrote the first history of the English people – and also, one hopes, had time for an occasional doze. Various powers have been attributed to the chair over the centuries – brides used to think sitting in the chair would guarantee they would have children.

Margaret's for short – at **King's Lynn** still has the sanctuary handle on the wicket of the west door which had only to be touched by a fugitive, so it is said, for him to gain temporary sanctuary within. Other churches however made it a little more difficult, such as the priory church at **Hexham** in Northumbria, where one had to get inside the building and sit on the sanctuary stool before being given the church's protection. The stool, which dates from before the Norman conquest, is still there.

At **Beverley** Minster on Humberside there was a further complication. The Minster also has a pre-Conquest sanctuary seat, where miscreants were offered an alternative to the usual 30 days' sanctuary followed by either trial or exile. If they gave all their property to the Crown and swore to become a servant of the Church, they could then live in Beverley, penniless but safe, for the rest of their lives. If they accepted this deal they became Frithmen; the stone sanctuary seat is called the Frith Stool. In the United States they might refer to this procedure as citing the Frith Amendment . . .

Beverley was the only place to offer this option. It is also one of the few to offer a convincing story of what could happen if sanctuary were violated. Local tradition has it that one of William the Conqueror's henchmen, called Toustain, was rash enough to pursue some rebellious townsfolk into the Minster. He was struck by a flash of lightning as he crossed the threshold and finished up with his head facing backwards and his limbs 'transformed to hideous lumps'. Nobody tried it again.

The ancient seat in St Paul's church, **Jarrow**, was not for sanctuary but for study. St Paul's has been called the cradle of English learning, and the straight-backed wooden chair is said to have belonged to the Venerable Bede, who spent most of his life in the monastery of which the original church formed a part. Seated in this chair Bede wrote the first history of the English people, translated the New Testament into the Saxon tongue, and occasionally, one hopes, put his feet up and had a doze. He is hailed as the father of English history and a pioneer of Bible translation. His home town has its own way of commemorating this great and gentle scholar; not far from St Paul's and that ancient chair is the Bede Industrial Estate . . .

The chair in the pulpit at the Tilehouse Baptist Church, Hitchin, was presented to the first pastor by John Bunyan.

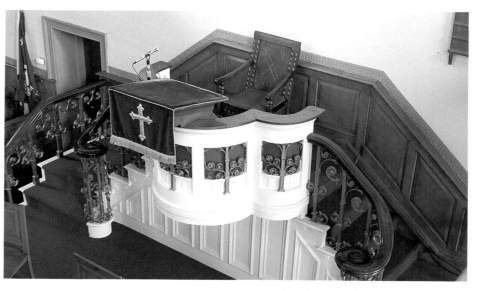

Birds of various feathers. An early explorer of the Americas introduced the turkey into Britain, particularly into Boynton Church; and a vicar with a passion for cock-fighting is said to have introduced the gamecock into Wednesbury Church.

Another famous chair can be found in the Tilehouse Baptist church in **Hitchin**, Hertfordshire. The chair was presented to the church's first pastor by John Bunyan, and now stands in the pulpit.

If an apparently mundane item of church furniture like a chair can have tales like these to tell, so can a lectern. Most lecterns, if they incorporate a decorative bird, favour an eagle, but St Bartholemew's church at **Wednesbury** in Staffordshire has a very belligerent gamecock rearing up and glaring at the congregation. One theory is that it was installed by a nineteenth-century vicar with a passion for cock-fighting, but other authorities estimate that the bird dates back to the fourteenth century – and maybe in those days, that was the way eagles looked.

The experts are in no doubt about the identity of the bird on the lectern of **Boynton** church, near Bridlington. It was put there in honour of William Strickland, who sailed to America with Sebastian Cabot in 1497 and claimed to be the first Englishman to set foot on American soil. He also introduced the American turkey to Europe, and it is undoubtedly a turkey with outspread tail which adorns the Boynton lectern, as well as the Strickland coat of arms in the east window. How long, I wonder, before Mr Bernard Matthews takes up the idea?

Church organs can have strange histories as well as church chairs and lecterns. **Tewkesbury** Abbey has no less than three organs, which must be a story in itself, but the most interesting is the Milton organ, which was made for Magdalen College, Oxford and reached Tewkesbury via Hampton Court. The abbey must be one of the few churches in the country which has reason to thank Oliver Cromwell, since it was he who first got the organ on the move. He had it taken from Oxford and installed in his Hampton Court quarters, where it is said that his secretary, John Milton, strummed the odd toccata on it for his master's delectation. The name has stuck ever since.

The organ of St John's church, **Wolverhampton**, has also travelled extensively, but it was never intended to come to rest in Wolverhampton. It was built by Renatus Harris for Christ Church cathedral in Dublin in about 1683. In due course it was replaced by a new one and the organ-builder who supplied the replacement took the old one away in part exchange. He only got it as far as Wolverhampton when he was taken ill and died. His widow decided not to move it any further – a full-size church organ is not the easiest or cheapest item to cart around the country – and she sold it to the nearest church, which happened to be St John's, for £500.

The much-travelled organ of St John's Church, Wolverhampton was on its way from Dublin to London when its owner died.

The much-travelled altar at Burnham-on-Sea, which came there via Whitehall Palace, Hampton Court and Westminster Abbey, has a reredos by Inigo Jones. The church tower looks more like Over-i-go than Inigo; it is three feet out of the vertical.

At **Burnham-on-Sea** in Somerset it is not the church organ which has been on tour but the so-called Whitehall altar, with its seventeenth-century marble cherubs in various attitudes of rapture and devotion, and all looking terribly cute. The reredos was designed by Inigo Jones and made by Grinling Gibbons for James II, to go in the chapel of Whitehall Palace. When the building was burned down it was removed to Hampton Court – which seems to have been a popular clearing house for surplus church furnishings – and thence to Westminster Abbey. In 1820 George IV, whose attitude to churches was not always as belligerent as they might have thought in Guildford, presented it to Bishop King of Rochester, who was also Vicar of Burnham.

The other unusual feature about Burnham church, incidentally, is its 80-foot tower, which leans 3 feet out of the vertical – not easy to spot with the naked eye but enough to make any civil engineer shudder. Happily it has stayed that way for a long time, and shows no sign of leaning any further.

There are so many stained glass windows in our urban churches in memory of remarkable people that I hesitate to single any out, but there is one which is remarkable just for the sheer number of famous people it commemorates – all of them women. In **High Wycombe**, Buckinghamshire, better known for furniture than feminism, the parish church of All Saints' has a window portraying seventeen women who have made their mark in history. Not one of them, so far as I know, lived in High Wycombe, nor took a great deal of interest in it, but perhaps

they all passed that way in the course of their various activities. They range from Queen Victoria to Emily Brontë, from St Hilda and St Bridget to Elizabeth Fry and Florence Nightingale. The window was presented to the church – by a woman, of course – in 1933. Dame Frances Dove, by commemorating the famous in this way, has achieved a modest fame herself.

Even if a church lacks a fine window it can generally boast some fine carving. It does not have to be very grand or uplifting; medieval sculptors had a great sense of the workaday, as well as a sense of humour. The most entertaining of their creations are often found under the seats of misericords, where they would not normally be seen, so workmen were allowed a little extra licence. But at **Nantwich** church in Cheshire their bit of fun is in a prominent position outside the north transept. It is a sculpture of a woman with her hand in a pitcher, being caught by the Devil. The workmen apparently found their landlady helping herself to their money and decided to tell the world about it. Seven hundred years later, the world is still being told.

The Masons who built Nantwich church had their own back on a landlady they found stealing their money from a pitcher; she has been caught by the Devil.

Let us now praise famous *women*. The stained glass window at High Wycombe has a distinguished assortment, from Emily Brontë to Florence Nightingale.

Medieval graffiti at Ashwell.
Translation: 'The quoins are not
joined aright – I spit at them.'

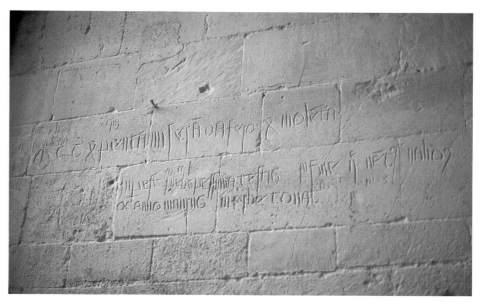

Rather more serious wall
decorations at Newark-on-Trent;
one of the few illustrations in
an English church of the
medieval Dance of Death.

Although they were working in church,
medieval masons were not above leaving
a little graffiti on the walls. There is still
some visible at **Leighton Buzzard** in Bedfordshire, though it is difficult to
appreciate the full force of it after so
many years. But there is no doubt,
according to some experts, about the
meaning of a comment on the wall of St
Mary's church at **Ashwell** in Hertfordshire. It may look indecipherable, but I
am told it must have been put there by a
mason who was disgusted by the poor
workmanship of his colleagues. It is said
to read: 'The quoins are not joined aright
– I spit at them'.

Of course not all church wall decorations are quite so down-to-earth. St Mary
Magdalene church at **Newark-on-Trent**
has one of the few illustrations still exist-
ing in an English church of the Dance of
Death. A medieval painting on the wall of
the Markham Chantry Chapel shows
Death, in the form of a skeleton, offering a
rose with two buds to an elegantly clad
figure in red and black coat and jewelled
velvet hat. It demonstrates how death
comes even to the noblest and the richest,
a favourite theme of medieval mortality
plays and church paintings, but I know
of only one other such painting in
an English church, in the choir of
Hexham Abbey.

One has to add that it is not all doom and gloom in St Mary Magdalene's. There are some quite jolly carvings elsewhere in the church, of owls and lions and lizards. And don't forget to look under those misericord seats . . .

Apart from the windows and the decorations, another fascinating feature of many town churches is the font. It can have the most elaborate and unlikely carvings, but the one I plump for is at **Tunbridge Wells**, in the church of King Charles the Martyr, not because of how it looks but how it received its own baptism. The church, like the rest of seventeenth-century Tunbridge Wells, was built in most elegant style for the fashionable folk who came down from London to take the waters. One might expect that the first child to be baptised in the smart new font would be a baby viscount or an infant earl, but the story goes that it was first used for the child of a gipsy-woman who happened to be passing through the town.

Was the vicar generous of heart and unmindful of social distinctions? Or did he just want a trial run with the new font before coping with the gentry?

Not even the elegance of Tunbridge Wells can compete with the luxury of St Mary's, **Axminster**. The first impression is more of a stately drawing-room than a parish church. The pews are set back so one gets the full benefit of a vast expanse of magnificent Axminster carpet. The earliest Axminsters were made in 1775 in a building just beside the church by Thomas Whitty, who had picked up the technique from the Turks. It is said that each time he finished a carpet the church bells were rung in celebration – or perhaps because the church council thought, 'This one's for us'. They got it in the end.

At Axminster, even the parish church has its Axminster carpet. Each time the factory next door produced a new carpet they rang the church bells in celebration.

The most interesting feature of some churches can be seen without even entering the building; they go in for very fancy gateways. At **Kirkby Stephen** in Cumbria the fairly undramatic church of St Stephen has a most ostentatious colonnaded entrance where a modest lych-gate would normally be. There is a painted stone portico supported by eight columns, and on top of it a bell, a globe, a cross – the lot. This awesome edifice, which dominates the main street of the town, was given by a naval purser, one John Waller, who left instructions about it in his will. Mr Waller had obviously done quite nicely out of naval pursering and felt he should add a dash of tone to his home town, but his legacy might look better on a Greek hillside than in the heart of the Cumbrian moors.

Ashbourne church in Derbyshire has an eye-catching gateway too, though not quite so overwhelming. The pillars of the wrought-iron gates are topped by flaming cones, and the cones are held up by four skulls – a grim foretaste of what lies in the churchyard beyond.

The peculiarity of **Crediton**'s 'Royal Peculiar' church lies in the Governors' Room in the Chapter House. The church

Not just another lych-gate for Kirkby Stephen church, but colonnades, a bell, a globe and a cross (below). Nor for Ashbourne church, where the tops of the gate pillars are held up by skulls (below, right).

The Governors' Room at Crediton's 'Royal Peculiar' church has its own peculiarities – roof beams made from ships' timbers, and a floor made from a single elm tree.

was granted a royal charter by Edward VI, under which it is run by a board of governors, and the room where they meet has a floor cut from a single elm tree, a quite splendid expanse of wood, albeit a trifle uneven, which dates back 700 years. The roof beams are unusual too; they were originally ships' timbers.

Blackpool is not particularly noted for its churches – it has a 7-mile prom, a 500-foot tower, 26 bowling greens, 2 golf courses, 16 children's playgrounds, 3 piers, a rose garden with 30,000 blooms and a conservatory with 700 species of chrysanthemum, but we know much less about its places of worship. Those that it does have are not very ancient, including All Hallows', which was rebuilt in the last century, but it has retained its old Norman porch. Around the doorway, unexpectedly, are the signs of the zodiac, carved many centuries before the first fortune-teller set up a stall on the Golden Mile.

All Hallows' church, Blackpool had signs of the zodiac round the door long before they started telling fortunes with them on the Golden Mile.

Reminders of earlier invasions – by floodwaters at King's Lynn, where the church warns of when to expect high tides (above and above, right), and by Mithraic worshippers at Wigan parish church (below and right).

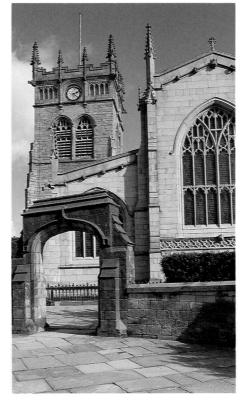

The entrance to St Margaret's, **King's Lynn**, bears marks of more recent significance. They are high water marks outside the west door, which used to be close by the River Ouse before it changed course, and at times of flood has seen its return. The earliest mark was in 1883 and the highest, not as I expected in 1953, the year of the great East Coast floods, but more recently in 1978. On each occasion the water swept through the church to a depth of 4 or 5 feet.

High above the west door is St Margaret's unique early warning system, the seventeenth-century moon clock, on which a dragon on a revolving central disc points to the time of the next high tide. Instead of numbers the hours are indicated by letters, which I thought at first sight must spell the name of the lady who had presented it: Edith Gihnnyl. I discovered however that the actual benefactor was a gentleman called Thomas Tue; I had been reading the letters backwards . . .

St Margaret's dates back to the first Norman bishop of Norwich, who built the priory church and called the little settlement Lynn Episcopi – Bishop's Lynn. One might think that must pre-date anything to be found in **Wigan**, which according to popular mythology has only one historic monument, Wigan Pier. But the parish church of All Saints' contains a relic from a much earlier age than the Normans. It is the remains of a Mithraic stone altar, discovered during the 1850s when the church was being restored. As there was already an altar in the standard position the church council had to find another home for it, and rather curiously they chose to set the stone into the surround of one of the windows in the tower.

The stone in the north aisle of St Cuthbert's church in **Bedlington**, Northumberland, has a rather different significance. It is inscribed 'Watson's Wake', and it commemorates an unfortunate seventeenth-century somnambulist called Cuthbert Watson. Mr Watson was not only a sleep-walker, he was a sleep-climber. He was halfway up one of the buttresses of the church when a passer-by gave a shout. He woke with a start – and fell to his death. I am not sure whether 'Watson's Wake' refers to his unhappy awakening or the proceedings after his funeral, since the official church guide, which goes into much detail about how the body of St Cuthbert once rested there en route to Durham, omits any mention of his hapless namesake.

Mr Watson has achieved less prominence, in fact, than a humble beggar whose life-size effigy occupies a commanding position in St John's parish church, **Halifax**, and who gets much publicity in the church literature. He is universally known as Old Tristram, though he has also been referred to as Trosteram, a member of a local shoe-making family. There is also disagreement over the date of the effigy; it is inscribed 1701, but the clothing indicates it could have been half a century earlier. It does seem generally agreed, however, that Old Tristram was licensed to beg in the church porch representing the poor of the parish. He still holds out a collecting box on their behalf.

Finally, the bells and clocks of our town churches. What is believed to be the

'Watson's Wake', in memory of a rude awakening at Bedlington.

oldest church turret clock in England still worked by its original mechanism was made in Winchelsea in 1560 for St Mary's church, **Rye**. The massive pendulum still swings inside the church, and outside by the clock face are two pugnacious

Old Tristram, who has collected for the poor at St John's church, Halifax for nearly three centuries.

cherubs, scantily clad in small pieces of curtaining, who punch the bell on the quarter-hours. The inscription reminds us sombrely:

For our time is a very shadow that passeth away.

Christ Church, **Bristol**, also has a clock with quarter-jacks striking the bells on each side, but strangely these muscular figures do not actually belong to the church. They are leased from Bristol Corporation for thirteen pence a year, which must make them the lowest valued council workers in the country.

St Michael's church in **Beccles**, Suffolk, also did an interesting deal with the local authority. The bell tower which was built next to the church in the sixteenth century was sold to Beccles town council in 1972 for one penny; the actual coin is embedded in a plaque on the wall. The tower was not quite the bargain it may seem; the plaque records that the council then had to raise £68,000 to restore it.

Most of the tunes which church clocks play are familiar, and none more so than the clock of Great St Mary's in **Cambridge**, the official university church. As you listen to it, you may think you are in Westminster or tuned in to the BBC. The chimes were specially written for St Mary's in 1793, but they became known throughout the world when they were copied for the clock we call Big Ben . . .

One way to spend a penny: in Beccles it bought the church bell tower for the council. But not the bargain it may seem – they had to raise £68,000 to restore it.

Church clocks with striking features: England's oldest church turret clock at Rye (top), municipal quarter-jacks at Bristol (above) and a very familiar chime in Cambridge (right).

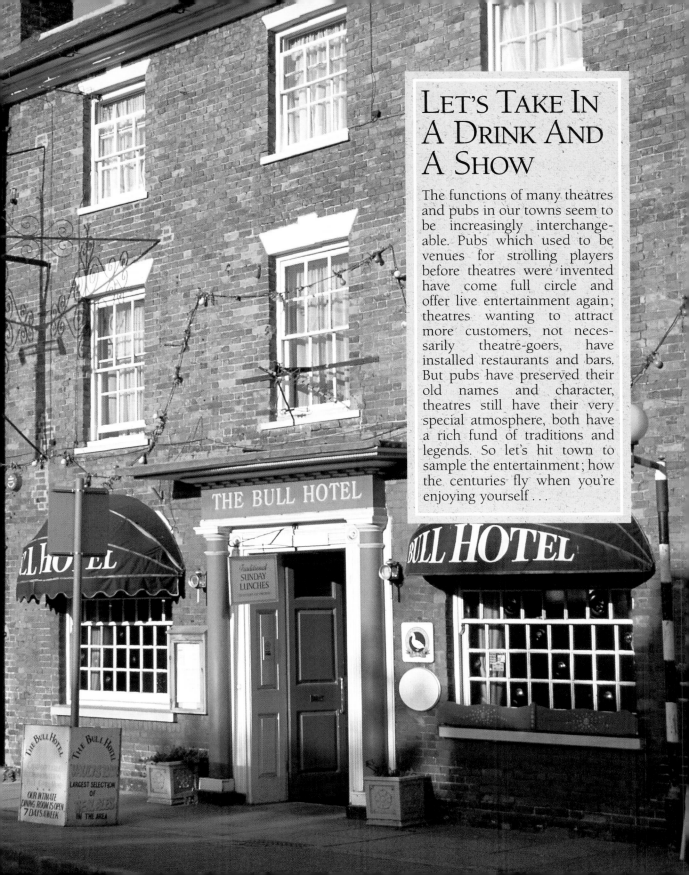

LET'S TAKE IN A DRINK AND A SHOW

The functions of many theatres and pubs in our towns seem to be increasingly interchangeable. Pubs which used to be venues for strolling players before theatres were invented have come full circle and offer live entertainment again; theatres wanting to attract more customers, not necessarily theatre-goers, have installed restaurants and bars. But pubs have preserved their old names and character, theatres still have their very special atmosphere, both have a rich fund of traditions and legends. So let's hit town to sample the entertainment; how the centuries fly when you're enjoying yourself . . .

THE BULL HOTEL

The development of public entertainment: a purpose-built cockpit at Welshpool (right), a pub courtyard for strolling players in Gloucester (below) . . .

. . . and a Georgian theatre in Bristol (right), built to take an audience of 1600.

Even before the days of strolling players, provincial inns offered a form of live entertainment – though half the performers were dead at the end of it. Cock-fighting was a great draw for the customers, sometimes in the yard, sometimes in the pub itself. At the Ketton Ox at **Yarm** in Cleveland, for instance, they staged the fights in an upper room. When cock-fighting was made illegal a trapdoor was installed as an emergency exit in case they were raided.

Welshpool in Powys has preserved a free-standing cockpit, a brick building with ten high windows which was erected specifically for that purpose. It was later put to various uses and fell into disrepair in the 1970s, but it has now been restored with its six-sided pit in the centre, and around it the ledges and alcoves where the bets were laid. It looks very functional and business-like, more suited to a classroom than a cock-fight.

One of the earliest inns to double as a theatre was the New Inn at **Gloucester**, which like so many 'New Inns' is very old indeed. It was built around 1457 to cater for the pilgrims who poured into the city to visit Edward II's tomb. It still has the stone-flagged courtyard where the players performed at one end and the peasantry watched from the other, in what was called 'the pit', while the more favoured customers looked down from the galleries and windows.

When purpose-built theatres reached the provinces in the eighteenth century they followed the same pattern, with a pit and balconies, but eventually the social categories were reversed: the carriage trade went into the stalls and the lower orders were banished to the 'gods'.

The link between pubs and theatres is well illustrated by the building of the Georgian theatre in **Penzance**. A local paper announced in 1786: 'The Ship and Castle Inn, Penzance, wishes to announce that an elegant theatre is about to be built by the Manager of the Exeter Company of Comedians in the yard behind the house'. No doubt in due course the locals patronised both.

The Penzance theatre was one of several in the West Country which were built and managed by Richard Hughes, often called the father of provincial drama. It was dismantled in 1839 and had a varied career as a billiard hall, a Masonic Lodge, a meeting room, an ice-house, a furniture store, a workshop and a Brownie headquarters. Only the stage and part of the boxes and gallery survived all these metamorphoses, but in 1986 the Friends of the Georgian Theatre came into being. They cleared out the rubbish and debris, stripped away much of the later alterations, and set off on the long, long road to restoration.

The Theatre Royal in **Richmond**, in Yorkshire, another of the earliest provincial theatres, went through the same sort of experience as the one in Penzance. After being closed down it was used as an auction room, a shop, a warehouse and a salvage depot – though it did escape the Brownies. But the Friends came to its rescue much earlier, and they completed its restoration in 1962. The seating capacity of the pit, originally 400, was reduced to a more comfortable 229, but the boxes and galleries remain virtually unchanged.

Bristol's Theatre Royal was built on a larger scale, to accommodate an audience of 1600. Garrick called it 'the most complete of its dimensions in England', which makes no obvious sense but is clearly meant to be complimentary. It was first called merely 'The Theatre in King Street' because it had no licence, and it took 12 years to overcome the objections of the more puritanical Bristolians, before a patent was granted and the theatre became officially Royal.

Norwich also had a Theatre Royal, built in 1758, but it was burned down in the thirties and only the name remains on the present building. However the city does have another theatre which looks as though it has even earlier origins, in the style of an Elizabethan playhouse. Actually, the Maddermarket, named after the old market where dyestuffs were sold in medieval times, has only been a theatre since 1921. Before that it was a Roman Catholic chapel, which became

A genuine early theatre at Richmond, now restored (below) and a not-so-genuine Elizabethan theatre in Norwich, the Maddermarket, which was a Roman Catholic chapel until 1921 (bottom).

redundant. It was converted by Nugent Monck, a great figure in the Norwich theatre who had been directing amateur productions since before the First World War, and planned to produce all of Shakespeare's plays in these appropriate surroundings. His actors were always anonymous, and the tradition continues today.

While Norwich has a theatre which seems straight out of the sixteenth century, **Manchester** has one which seems straight out the twenty-first. It is another remarkable conversion job, this time starting with an old cotton exchange and creating the theatre within a steel capsule inside the walls of the old building. There was plenty of room to play with, since the old exchange covered an acre of floor space and was claimed in the 1920s, when it was built, to be 'the biggest room in the world'. The floor was not strong enough to bear the weight of the steel structure, so it was suspended from the hall's marble columns, with flights of steps leading down to ground level, making it look rather like a spaceship about to disgorge its alien crew. It actually disgorges up to 700 theatre-goers after each performance.

Just as disconcerting as finding a spaceship in an old cotton exchange is finding an elegant Victorian theatre in an old stone castle. It was the creation of Madame Adelina Patti, the opera singer who was born in Madrid of Italian parents, grew up in New York, toured the great cities of the world, and finished up in **Swansea**. She bought Craigynos Castle at the top of Swansea Valley and added her own private theatre, with fluted pillars, plaster decorations in pink, yellow and gold, and a floor which could be ingeniously tilted for a sloping auditorium, or laid flat for a ballroom. On the stage curtain is a painting of Dame Patti driving a chariot in her famous role of Rossini's 'Seramide'.

Considering the historic connections between pubs and theatres there are surprisingly few such paintings of great performers on inn signs. Kings and queens, saints and soldiers, explorers, fliers, mountaineers – but where are all the stage stars? Singers are represented by the Jenny Lind at **Hastings** and another in **Sutton**, though she was born in Sweden and died in Malvern, and her name was actually Madame Goldschmidt. Perhaps Lady Godiva qualifies as an entertainer; she appears discreetly on a pub sign in **Coventry**. But otherwise, outside the West End, I can only offer more tenuous links, like the Dog Tray Inn at **Brighton**. It sounds like a canine sanitary device, but it was the name of a music-hall sketch about a dog called Tray, which

A space-age theatre inside an old corn exchange in Manchester. Would you suspect that both these pictures are of the same building?

is ill-treated by its master but gets the last laugh. The full story, appropriately in doggerel verse, appears on a plaque in the bar.

Then there is the Showman at **Cullompton** in Devon, which has a sign depicting a fairground operative with a two-headed dwarf, or the Drum and Monkey at **Stamford**, which also sounds as if it has a fairground connection but it only got the name in the 1950s, and not many drum-playing monkeys were performing in Stamford then.

That brings us to the oddities and unexpected meanings of pub names and signs. In a town these can often be the only interesting features of an otherwise characterless establishment, and it can be difficult to spot the pub's actual name among the assortment of signs for Chefs and Brewers, Toby Pantries, Falstaff Inns and the like. When you do spot it, the name does not always tally with the sign, unless you know the story behind it.

Take the Snowdrop Inn at **Lewes** in Sussex. It is not the familiar white flower that appears on the sign, but a snow scene with drifts up to chimney height and men probing the snow with long sticks. It recalls a grim Christmas eve in 1836, when an avalanche of snow and ice, a lethal 'snowdrop', came down the hill above the pub and demolished a row of cottages, killing eight people.

Surprises on the hillsides: The Snowdrop Inn is named not after a flower, but an avalanche.

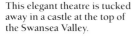

This elegant theatre is tucked away in a castle at the top of the Swansea Valley.

Inn sign oddities. Harlow's pubs are named after butterflies, with a punned version of the name on the other side (above). The Sun at Yeovil could be a giant chrysanthemum chasing a horseman (right). The Triple Plea at Halesworth portrays a devilish argument (below, right).

Similarly the Dairy Maid at **Aylesbury** in Buckinghamshire does not have a buxom country wench on its sign but a stage-coach which bore that name. It passed through the town on its way from London to Buckingham and brought the news of Wellington's victory at Waterloo. The pub itself can't claim to have witnessed the celebrations – it was only built in 1966.

The Bulldog in **Oxford** has nothing to do with dogs, but with the officials who police the university, while the Mitre at

The Sun

FREE HOUSE

THE TRIPLE PLEA

Tonbridge in Kent is linked not with a bishop but with the church of King Charles the Martyr; the spelling has changed over the years. Similarly it is a confusion over pronunciation which has produced the Dog and Bacon at **Horsham**; it is a corruption of Dorking Beacon, a local landmark.

There are some financial eccentricities on pub signs. At Ancoats in **Manchester** there is the Bank of England, not a branch of the Old Lady of Threadneedle Street but named in honour of a former landlord (and no doubt it applies equally to the present one) in recognition of his honesty. The Old Crown at **Hayes** in Middlesex has nothing to do with monarchs, though it does have a link with sovereigns; the sign depicts an old five-shilling piece. And the delightfully named Tinker and Budget at **Oswaldtwistle** in Lancashire, which could so easily have been a dig at the Chancellor, refers to a quite different budget, the little sack on a stick which travellers carried over their shoulder.

The sign of the Sun Inn at **Yeovil** is a little confusing too. It shows a dashing young chap standing upright on two horses, with what looks like a giant chrysanthemum in the background. It was painted by a well-known inn sign artist, Stanley Chew, who perhaps got bored with painting straightforward suns and threw in Apollo for a bit of variety.

It was not boredom but lack of planning that led to the sign of the Tommy Ducks in **Manchester**. The pub was originally called Princes, after a nearby theatre (there's the theatrical link again), but an extrovert landlord decided that he wanted to feature on the sign too. His name was Tommy Duckworth. Halfway through his surname the sign-writer ran out of sign, and the Princes became Tommy Ducks.

A dancing bear is not unusual on an inn sign, but I know of only one Balancing Eel, at **South Shields** in Tyne and Wear. It shows a sailor with an eel balanced on his nose. There is no theatrical link here, alas. It merely illustrates a poem about an old man whose eye was as steady as ever – 'he balanced an eel on the end of his nose – what made him so awfully clever?'

Another poem is illustrated at the Triple Plea Inn in **Halesworth** in Suffolk. The sign shows a lawyer, a doctor and a cleric arguing over a body with the Devil looking on. It takes quite a long poem to tell the whole story, but perhaps the first verse will suffice:

Law, Physic and Divinity,
Being in dispute could not agree,
To settle which among them three
Should have the superiority.

Needless to say, the Devil settles it for them.

When a new town pub is built, the search for a name can run into problems. The brewers were going to call their new pub at **Rickmansworth** in Hertfordshire the William Penn, in honour of the town's illustrious son – until it was pointed out that he was a lifelong teetotaller. The brewers admitted it was a fair cop and called it The Keystone instead.

On the other hand, when an entire collection of new pubs was built in **Harlow** they had the nice idea of naming them all after butterflies – and the even nicer idea of putting a punned version of the name on the other side of the sign. So at the White Admiral there is the butterfly on one side and a sailor on the other. The Garden Tiger has a cat; and so on. For the Small Copper they could have had a policeman, but they actually chose a farthing.

Whatever name a brewery may choose, the locals may decide to call it something quite different. At **Alnwick** in Northumberland there is a pub which is officially christened Ye Olde Cross but it is better known as the Dirty Bottles. This is not a slight on the landlord's standards of hygiene, but a reference to the old bottles in one of the windows. It is said that an earlier licensee was setting them out in the window recess some 150 years ago when he was struck down by some sinister illness and died. In case anyone touching the bottles was similarly stricken the window recess was sealed up on the inside, with the bottles still on display to passers-by. There they have remained, gathering layers of dust and cobwebs, ever since.

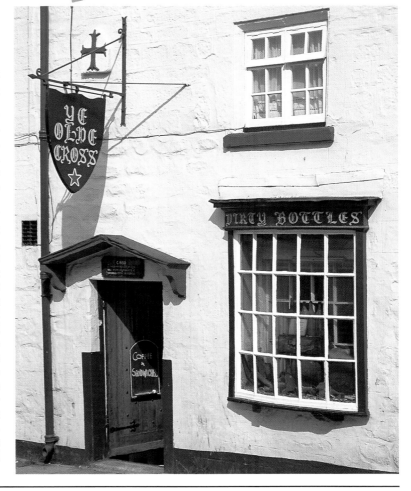

Ye Olde Cross at Alnwick became better known as the Dirty Bottles because of its unusual window display. The licensee died of some strange illness while arranging the bottles and nobody has touched them since.

The Cock and the Bull hotels at Stony Stratford gave a new phrase to the English language. Travellers' tales which were swapped in the bars were sometimes so far-fetched they became known as cock-and-bull stories.

There is a happier story behind the names of two old pubs at **Stony Stratford** in Buckinghamshire. One is the Cock, the other is the Bull. Both were popular coaching inns, where travellers swapped tales, which no doubt grew in the telling. Thus, so tradition has it, the cock-and-bull story came into being.

Sometimes it is the style of the actual sign which distinguishes a pub from its namesakes. In the Potteries town of **Tunstall** the Victoria Inn has the Queen's portrait picked out in mosaic tiles on the wall, while the George at **Stamford** has a sign extending across the road like a gallows, as a discouragement to highwaymen. The George is also very proud of its portrait of Daniel Lambert, who at 52 stone 11 lbs was the heaviest man ever to live in England. His walking stick, a medium-size tree trunk, is also on display. The actual link between Daniel and the George is not all that close. He was born in Leicester and only happened to be staying the night in Stamford when he suddenly died – not at the George but the Wagon and Horses, which no longer exists. However he is buried in Stamford churchyard, his clothes are in Stamford Museum, and no doubt the George felt it should have a share of the action.

There is no doubt about the historical significance of the George and Dragon at **Yarm** on Teesside. In 1820 in its Commercial Room the promoters met to set up the Stockton and Darlington Railway, the first public railway in the world. The railway reached Yarm soon afterwards, and the half-mile viaduct which carries it over the Tees still dominates the town.

The Victoria Inn at Tunstall (top) has an inn sign in the form of a mosaic on the wall. The George at Stamford (above, left) is rather more ostentatious. It also likes to remind people of its biggest customer, Daniel Lambert (above, right). The George and Dragon at Yarm may have had smaller customers, but the transport system they launched became very big indeed (left).

S.&.D.R.

IN THE COMMERCIAL ROOM OF THIS HOTEL, ON THE

12th Day of February, 1820

WAS HELD THE

PROMOTERS' MEETING

OF THE

Stockton & Darlington Railway-

THE FIRST PUBLIC RAILWAY IN THE WORLD.

THOMAS MEYNELL, ESQ., OF YARM, PRESIDED.

The Union Hotel in **Penzance** also claims a niche in history. It was in fact from a large niche in its diningroom – the minstrel's gallery – that the news was first announced in England of the death of Nelson at Trafalgar. The hotel's name, incidentally, is inspired by the Union Jack, not the TUC. Also in Penzance is the Admiral Benbow, which emphasises its nautical connection in a rather more obvious fashion. Lying on the roof is a full-size smuggler, in high red hat, blue jacket, heavy seaboots and a gun at the ready. His choice of look-out post is not ideal, since any Excise man would spot him from miles away, but as a publicity gimmick it is undeniably effective. Perhaps the Union Hotel will pick up the idea and have a full-size town crier permanently announcing Nelson's death up in its musicians' gallery.

Dick Turpin should have a full-size figure in nearly every pub between London and York, judging by the number which claim a connection with him, but one of the more authentic stories is told about him at the seventeenth-century Eight Bells Inn at **Hatfield** in Hertfordshire. It is said the Bow Street Runners were actually storming into the pub as Dick leaped from an upper window on to the back of his faithful Black Bess, making one of those crutch-jolting landings which happen all the time in Westerns but are still agony to watch. Dick escaped from Hatfield with everything still intact . . .

The Union Hotel in Penzance has a sign which is not connected with the TUC, it shows Lord Nelson and the Union Jack. It was from the gallery in the dining-room that the news was first announced in England of Nelson's death at Trafalgar.

A piece of industrial history is preserved at a couple of East Anglian pubs. The Bell at **Woodbridge** in Suffolk and the Fountain at **Soham** in Cambridgeshire each have a steelyard, a primitive wooden gantry with a hoist which was used for weighing cart-loads of wool or hides. And the Talbot Hotel in **Stow-on-the-Wold** has a rather smaller reminder of those days, a brass box on the front of the building in which farmers left packets of grain for the corn merchants to test for quality.

Reminders of earlier pub activities. A smuggler keeps watch for the Excise men on the roof of the Admiral Benbow in Penzance (above); the Fountain at Soham is equipped to weigh waggons (far left); and the Talbot at Stow-in-the-Wold has a brass box for corn samples (left and below).

Beams from the timbers of wrecked ships at Stratton (above), brick-barrel vaults at Wisbech, and a fourteenth-century vault under the George at Rochester (below).

Some pubs have historical curiosities built into them. The Tree at **Stratton** in Cornwall has beams made from the timbers of wrecked ships, the Rose and Crown at **Wisbech** has brick-barrel vaults dating from Tudor times, and the George at **Rochester**, built on the site of a church, has an even older vault going back to the fourteenth century. The King's Head at **Aylesbury** has an old stained-

glass window bearing the arms of Henry VI and Margaret of Anjou, while the Victoria at **Newnham** in Gloucestershire has a window dated 1622 which illustrates the fable of the grasshopper and the ant. It is actually a replica of the original, which amazingly was stolen from its frame some time ago.

The most handsomely decorated pub wall must be the front of the former White Hart Inn at **Newark-on-Trent**, twenty-four figures painted gold and blue against a red background. The pub no longer functions, but the façade is still beautifully preserved in its fifteenth-century glory above what is now a building society.

Ornamental curiosities: a stained glass window with the arms of Henry VI and Margaret of Anjou at the King's Head in Aylesbury (top), an illustrated fable at the Victoria, Newnham (left and above), and a fine array of figures on the wall of the former White Hart at Newark (left).

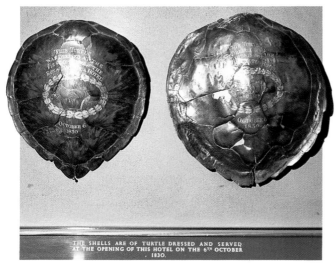

THE SHELLS ARE OF TURTLE DRESSED AND SERVED AT THE OPENING OF THIS HOTEL ON THE 6TH OCTOBER . 1830.

The Royal Victoria at Newport, Shropshire, is proud of its turtle shell (top), and the Bull's Head at Beaumaris is proud of its gateway with the largest single-hinge gate in Britain (above). The Grand Hotel at Scarborough used to be proud of its title as the biggest hotel in the country, but it has long since conceded defeat (right).

For an interior decoration nothing can quite match the Royal Victoria at **Newport** in Shropshire, which greets the traveller in its foyer with the shell of a monster turtle, 2 feet across. It was served when the hotel was opened in 1830. The Bull's Head at **Beaumaris**, Anglesey, also has an outsize offering, but this is in its courtyard, the largest single-hinge gate in Britain, 13 feet high and 11 feet wide.

This must lead to speculation about the largest inn in Britain, but who can distinguish these days between pubs, hotels, roadhouses and even motels, all of which have been known to call themselves 'inns'? When the Grand Hotel at **Scarborough** was built in 1867 it was not only the biggest in Britain but the biggest brick building in Europe. With a touch of whimsy it was given 365 rooms, 52 chimneys, 12 floors and 4 turrets. It has now lost its chimneys, its title and its atmosphere.

A more recent claimant was the Swan at Yardley in **Birmingham**, built a hundred years later. With eight bars, a restaurant, a steak bar, a banqueting room and a ballroom it was the ultimate in town pubs. Now it is down to just one bar, but the building still survives, about as big a contrast as you can imagine to the New Inn at Gloucester, where we began. But it does have one tenuous theatrical link; it is very nearly as ugly as the Royal Festival Hall.

NEVER MIND THE BOTTLE-NECK, FEEL THE BRIDGE

A waterway can help to give a town prosperity, but it is the bridges across the waterway which help to give it character. In a busy city this is not always easy to appreciate. To a motorist a bridge generally means a bottle-neck, and the more character it has, the more congestion it causes. It is difficult to savour the design of a medieval archway when it is reducing traffic to a single lane, and it is unwise to study a quaint inscription on the parapet when the 40-tonner behind you is nudging your rear bumper. But for those who seek the unusual aspects of a town, its bridges are often the place to look. And if it has an oddity to reveal or a tale to tell, then no bridge is too far.

Monnow bridge in **Monmouth** is a fair example of how one man's bottle-neck can be a more leisurely man's source of pleasure. It is Britain's only surviving fortified bridge; the thirteenth-century archway which stands on it was one of the four medieval gates to the town. For centuries it has been the main route into Monmouth, and although the gateway has been widened and a roof has been added in the shape of a Chinaman's hat, it offers much the same daunting appearance to the approaching motorist as it did to marauding cavalry when Henry V was born in the castle beyond.

But if you are a motorist in a hurry, take heart. There is now a bypass around Monmouth which crosses the river 600 yards away. With its two bridges, Monnow is now stereo . . .

The bridge at **Belper** in Derbyshire was also designed for defence, but under very different circumstances. The town grew up around the cotton mills of one Jebediah Strutt, who provided decent homes for those who worked for him, and gun embrasures on the bridge for those who didn't. It was a time of much rioting among the unemployed, and Jebediah made the bridge his first line of defence.

The medieval clergy were much inclined to use bridges as handy sites for chantries and chapels, so they could collect a few bob from passing travellers. Some survive even in the industrialised towns of the north. **Rotherham**, for instance, is better known for making brass in factories than taking brass on bridges, but the chapel of Our Lady still stands on the old four-arched bridge.

Monnow bridge at the entrance to Monmouth is Britain's only surviving fortified bridge (below) – unless you count Jebediah Strutt's bridge at Belper (below, right), which has gun embrasures to deal with unemployed rioters.

Wakefield claims to have the finest bridge chapel in England, but don't try to tell them that in Rotherham, where they have one too.

Mean-minded travellers will be relieved to know that it no longer functions as a chapel. It became an almshouse, then a prison, then remarkably a tobacconist's shop. And motorists in a hurry will also be glad to know that they don't have to squeeze across the old bridge any more; a new one was built in 1930.

The same thing has happened at **Wakefield**, where a new bridge bypasses the old bridge chapel of St Mary. It is said to be the finest of its kind in England – but don't trying saying that in Rotherham.

The bridge at **Henley-on-Thames** is familiar to vast numbers of tourists as well as rowing enthusiasts, but how many have paused to study it more closely? The stonework is decorated with masks of Father Thames and the goddess Isis, carved 200 years ago by a woman called Anne Damer. It is recorded that when she was not carving masks on bridges she was enjoying an early morning croissant with the Emperor Napoleon. But they don't talk about that sort of thing in Henley-on-Thames.

Another bridge to pause on is Bow Bridge in **Leicester**, to read the tablet which tells of the death of Richard III, who passed that way en route to Bosworth Field. It records that when a wise woman was asked if he would win the battle she said that where his spur struck, there his head would be broken.

This might have been a wise womanly way of saying he would fall head over heels off his horse, but as it turned out she meant it quite literally. As Richard rode off across the bridge his spur struck a stone. He returned in a much sorrier state, slung across the back of a horse, and as it carried him across the bridge his dangling head struck the same stone as his spur.

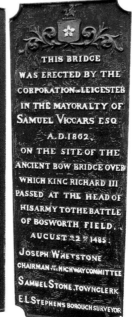

The plaques on Bow Bridge at Leicester tell it all.

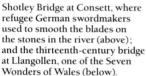
Shotley Bridge at Consett, where refugee German swordmakers used to smooth the blades on the stones in the river (above); and the thirteenth-century bridge at Llangollen, one of the Seven Wonders of Wales (below).

Pause also on Shotley Bridge at **Consett** in County Durham and look over the side into the River Derwent. Consett has been mainly known for its heavy engineering iron and steel works but in the seventeenth century it was famous for its swordmakers too. They were German refugees who settled by Shotley Bridge because the river water was ideal for tempering the blades. In the river you can still see the grooved stones on which they smoothed the steel.

In Wales you do not arrive on a bridge, of course, you come to the pont. The guidebooks will tempt you to come first to **Llangollen**, where the thirteenth-century stone bridge is acclaimed as one of the Seven Wonders of Wales – at least in Llangollen. But I prefer the old bridge at **Pontypridd**, not only because it is a very attractive bridge but because of the story behind it.

More accurately, Pontypridd should be spelt with a stutter in the middle, Pont-y-

ty-pridd, and a lisp at the end, prieth. Thus it sounds as if it ought to mean the 'bridge of the priest', and that is what it was. The man who put the pont in Pontypridd was the Rev. William Edwards, pastor of an Independent chapel who went in for designing bridges between services. Pontypridd was his first attempt, and many say his finest, but it was not all plain sailing. His first three bridges fell down, and it says much for the faith of the people who financed him (did they grant him a bridging loan?) that he was allowed to go on trying until he got it right.

He did so in an ingenious way. He decided his first three bridges were too heavy, so with the next one he left three holes on each side. This might well have weakened it so much that it fell down for a fourth time, but happily it held together and does so still – holes and all. Unfortunately he made it so steep that horses had great difficulty hauling anything over it, and they mostly continued using the ford until Pontypridd's second bridge – much less attractive but a lot more practical – was put up beside it a century later.

Rev. Edwards was undaunted by all this and went on building bridges with enormous enthusiasm all over Wales. There is one at **Dolauhirion**, not far from Llandovery, which is equally elegant on a smaller scale. Three of his sons also went into bridge building. But it is Pontypridd which is remembered best, and it is depicted on a slate tablet in the church porch at Eglwysilan, where William Edwards is buried.

The work of another enterprising Welsh bridge builder has not fared so well. In **Merthyr Tydfil**, home of the Cyfarthfa ironworks, once the biggest in the world, there was a bridge over the river made entirely of cast iron. It was built in 1800 by Watkin George, known as 'the mechanical genius of Cyfarthfa'. But when that part of the old town was cleared in 1966 and new housing was built by the river, the ageing cast-iron bridge was considered out of place. Genius or no, Watkin's bridge had to go. The last I heard, it had been dumped in Cyfarthfa Park.

Happily **Newport Pagnell** in Buckinghamshire has a more benevolent attitude to old iron bridges. It has preserved in Tickford Bridge the oldest one in Britain still in daily use. It was built just 10 years after Watkin George's in Merthyr Tydfil.

The Rev. William Edwards' bridge at Pontypridd – fourth time lucky!

Tickford Bridge is the oldest iron bridge in Britain still in daily use.

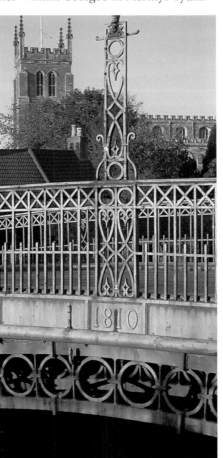

The only remaining transporter bridges in Britain. Newport's in Gwent used to carry six vehicles in its transporter car, but no longer functions (above). Middlesbrough on Teesside can take ten vehicles – and still does (below).

From Newport Pagnell to **Newport** in Gwent, and quite a different example of bridge building ingenuity, although it is no longer in use. It is a transporter bridge, the only one of its kind in Wales, and indeed there is only one other in Britain. You could not walk or drive across it, you travelled in a transporter car suspended from a platform which spans the river, between two towers which are nearly 250 feet high. The transporter car is reminiscent of a mountain cable car but much bigger; it could take six vehicles and quite a lot of people.

It is reached via Brunel Street, but it was not built by the ubiquitous Isambard. The designer was a Frenchman who put up a similar bridge in Marseilles. From 1906 until a few years ago the transporter car ran at regular intervals from 5.30 am until 11 pm free of charge. And you could climb one of the towers for threepence.

Britain's other transporter bridge is larger than Newport's and still working. It

was built in **Middlesbrough** on Teesside in 1911 and looks like two giant derricks jutting out from each side of the river and meeting in the middle. It is an unlovely structure but remains one of the more interesting features of this steel and petrochemical town. The bridge is the biggest of its kind in the world, capable of carrying ten cars compared with Newport's six, together with 600 passengers – though that must be quite a squeeze. If you are eager to get an extensive view of industrial Teesside there is no better vantage point, 160 feet above the Tees.

You may prefer the view from **Marlow** suspension bridge, which links Berkshire and Buckinghamshire. It is a baby brother of the very similar bridge which links Buda and Pest in Hungary, designed by the same man, William Tierney Clark. While the Danube is definitely not blue the Thames quite often is, and now that a new dual carriageway bypasses Marlow the old suspension bridge is an ideal and fairly peaceful spot to admire one of the loveliest stretches of the river. You can also admire the garden of the Compleat Angler, though to patronise this famous riverside hostelry it helps to be a Compleat Millionaire . . .

In the rich sheep-farming areas of Britain it used to be said that a church or a manor house, or even a town hall, had been built on wool. In Cornwall there is a bridge which actually was. The splendid medieval bridge at **Wadebridge**, built in 1468, has the piers of its thirteen arches set on massive packs of wool sunk into the river-bed. They believed it would provide greater strength and stability, and as the bridge still stands after 500 years they were probably right.

Marlow Bridge (above) is a smaller version of the bridge which links Buda and Pest across the Danube. The medieval bridge at Wadebridge (below) has its piers set on massive packs of wool in the riverbed.

The Devil's Bridge at Kirkby Lonsdale was said to have been built by the Devil in return for the soul of the first creature to cross it. He was expecting the old woman who had to cross it to reach her cattle – but she sent her dog across first.

The money to build the bridge was raised by a vicar of Wadebridge, Thomas Lovibond, because he thought the ferry was too dangerous. Quite the reverse procedure happened at **Kirkby Lonsdale** in Cumbria, where a fourteenth-century vicar, far from contributing to the bridge, was awarded a grant of portage, a toll which had to be paid to him by travellers who used it. One might expect it to be called the Vicar's Bridge, but it has always been known as the Devil's Bridge, thanks to the tale of the Crafty Crone of Kirkby.

The Crafty Crone lived beside the river before any bridge existed. She kept her cattle on the far side and reached them by wading across. When the river was swollen by rain and she could not cross it, the Devil offered to build her a bridge overnight if she gave him the soul of the first creature who crossed it. In the morning the Devil waited for her to cross it and thus forfeit her soul, but the Crafty Crone threw a bun across the bridge and her dog pursued it to the other bank. The Devil disappeared in a fury, the crone reached her cattle, the dog ate its bun, a local bard wrote a poem about it and Kirkby Lonsdale Tourist Association has kept the story going ever since.

To be fair, the town guide admits there is quite a different explanation for the bridge's name. It is still attributed to the Devil, but in this version he was going to build it anyway, and indeed planned a much grander, wider one, regardless of any crones. However, as he was flying over Casterton Fell with a load of stones in his apron the apron-strings broke and he dropped most of them on the Fell. He had to make do with what were left, which is why the bridge is so narrow. As proof of this tale, of course, one can find a great many stones scattered about on Casterton Fell. But supporters of the Crafty Crone will point out the Devil's neck collar 200 yards downstream, which he flung off in his rage after she had fooled him. It is a big circular hole in a block of limestone, and it is as easy to picture the Devil wearing that as wearing an apron . . .

One might have expected, with such strange tales attached to it, that the Devil's Bridge would be haunted, but not even the local tourist office claims that. There are in fact very few haunted bridges of any note, but you may feel an odd shiver as you cross St Mary's bridge in **Derby**. It has one of those bridge chapels I referred to earlier, but it also has a grim tale attached to it. Derby may not be a city to associate with ghostly hauntings; it has more to do with Rolls-Royce and railways. But back in 1588 it saw its share of religious persecution, and on St

Bridges of sadness. On St Mary's Bridge in Derby were displayed the severed limbs of martyred priests (left). The Bridge of Sighs at Chester was used by condemned men on their way to execution (below, left). On Cobham bridge Queen Matilda mourned the drowning of a lady-in-waiting (below).

Mary's bridge there were displayed the severed limbs of three Roman Catholic priests who died gruesomely for their faith. It is said that on certain nights you can still hear their screams as their arms were torn from their bodies.

Similarly you may still hear a sigh or two on the bridge in **Chester** which crosses the canal outside Northgate. It is indeed known as the Bridge of Sighs, because this was the route taken by con-demned men from their dungeon to the chapel of Little St John, to take their final sacrament. And on **Cobham** bridge in Surrey you may hear the weeping of Queen Matilda, wife of Henry I, as she mourns the death of one of her hand-maidens who was drowned at this spot.

Enough of disappointed Devils and dismembered dissenters, of convicted criminals and crying queens. Let us move on to a later breed of bridge, the product

A bridge with a hole in it, at Worcester (above) and a bridge with an echo in it, the Sounding Arch at Maidenhead (below).

Isambard Kingdom Brunel, railway bridge builder extraordinary, had no such qualms over economy. He used as many bricks as he felt inclined when he built the railway bridge over the Thames at **Maidenhead**. Its two arches are the widest and flattest brick arches in the world, each one spanning 128 feet with a rise of only 24 feet, which may not mean much to a layman but I gather to an engineer is quite remarkable. One result was a dramatic echo, which gave the bridge the name of the Sounding Arch. If Brunel had saved on bricks and left a lot of holes one wonders if the echo would have been lost. If not, they might have named it the Sounding Cheese . . .

One of the few wooden railway bridges which still survive is at **Barmouth** in Gwynedd. It is not so much a bridge, more a viaduct, half a mile long, with an iron swing bridge at one end. It carries the Cambrian Coast line across the Mawddach estuary, and comes in handy as a foot-bridge too.

A foot-bridge which looks sturdy enough to carry a railway was built just after the First World War in **Swansea**, so that pedestrians could safely cross the coast road and two railway lines to reach the beach. It has been likened to a miniature Sydney Harbour bridge, which

of the railway age. Surprisingly there is one which uses the same principle that William Edwards did to stop the last of his Pontypridd bridges from collapsing. It crosses the canal and the road at **Worcester** on two brick arches, unlike Mr Edwards' single span, and being a railway bridge it is flat on top, which might take him aback, but he would recognise the big hole which has been left over one of the arches. It is there to reduce the weight of the brickwork, just like his holes at Pontypridd – and also, being built by a thrifty Victorian, to save money.

is pushing it a bit, but now that holiday-makers have cars and mostly head for the Gower if they are looking for sea and sand, this grand structure does seem a little excessive.

At the other extreme there is a very modest little foot-bridge in **Hungerford**, Berkshire, which nevertheless is regarded as one of the town's odder tourist attractions. It links the High Street with the first-floor entrance of a house called Bridge Gardens. The Kennet and Avon Canal passes the house and you might think the bridge was built to span it, but underneath it there is an entrance drive and another front door. In fact there seems no real need for the bridge at all; it was added in Regency times to the much older house, presumably as a short cut from street level.

All bridges great and small: the half-mile wooden viaduct at Barmouth (above), the outsize pedestrian bridge to the beach at Swanage (below, left) and the tiny footbridge to a front door at Hungerford (below).

The longest pedestrian escalator in Europe (above) which leads to the foot-tunnel under the Tyne at Jarrow. So far it seems to have escaped the aerosol paint-sprayers of the London Underground, and could make history as Britain's cleanest escalator. The bridge across Alum Chine (right) could have had a place in history also, if the young man who foolhardily jumped off it had not survived.

Before leaving foot-bridges I must mention a remarkable foot-tunnel. Most river tunnels are designed for motor traffic, and such are the fumes that no pedestrian would want to be seen dead in them – which is probably the only way he would. But occasionally one finds a river tunnel solely for walkers, and there is one alongside the main Tyne Tunnel which links **Jarrow** with the north bank. It has the distinction of being entered by the longest pedestrian escalator in Europe. Even more remarkable, the escalator is kept immaculate. There are no advertisements to be scribbled on and the blank surfaces are graffiti-free. That at least was my last view of it; by now it may have succumbed to aerosol paint sprayers like those who haunt the London Underground.

Finally a fairly ordinary bridge which might have played the central role in changing the course of history. It is the little suspension bridge which crosses Alum Chine in **Bournemouth**. In 1893 a youth was being chased in a game with young relatives. They trapped him in the centre of the bridge, and being something of a show-off he evaded them by jumping into the branches of the pine trees below. Unfortunately the branches were further away than he thought. They failed to hold him and he dropped 30-odd feet to the ground. It could easily have killed him; as it was he was unconscious for 3 days, then had to spend 3 months in bed with a ruptured kidney.

His name was Winston Churchill.

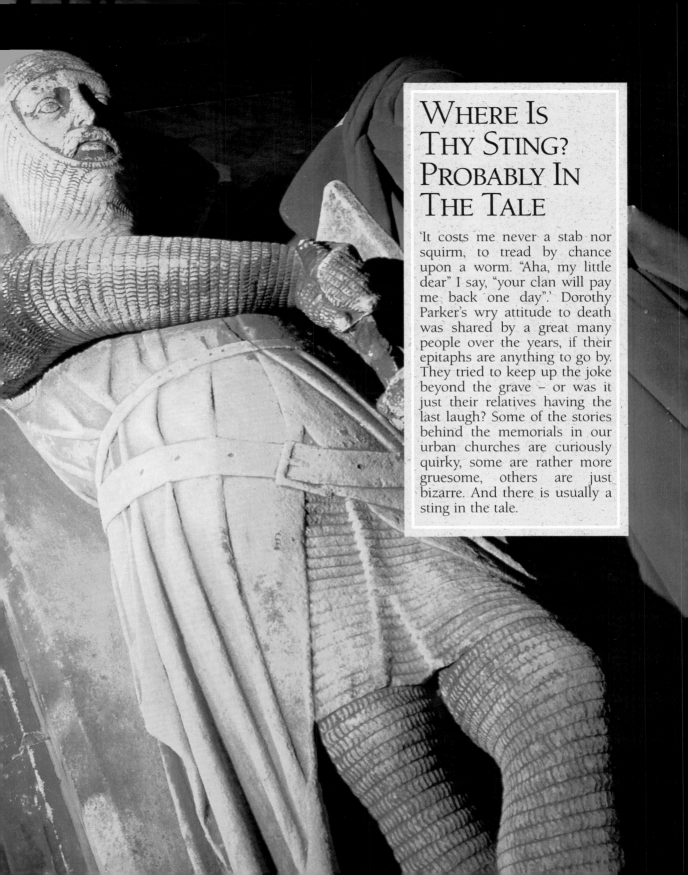

WHERE IS THY STING? PROBABLY IN THE TALE

'It costs me never a stab nor squirm, to tread by chance upon a worm. "Aha, my little dear" I say, "your clan will pay me back one day".' Dorothy Parker's wry attitude to death was shared by a great many people over the years, if their epitaphs are anything to go by. They tried to keep up the joke beyond the grave – or was it just their relatives having the last laugh? Some of the stories behind the memorials in our urban churches are curiously quirky, some are rather more gruesome, others are just bizarre. And there is usually a sting in the tale.

The oldest epitaphs still in existence must be those hieroglyphics left by the ancient Egyptians in honour of their dead Pharaohs. We have to jump a couple of thousand years before it occurred to the British that it might be a nice idea to say a few kind words on a tombstone about the dear departed.

In Wales the earliest evidence of this – indeed the earliest example of written Welsh – is in the little town of **Tywyn** in Gwynedd. Tywyn is a seaside resort, but only just. It was inland until a salt magnate from Droitwich decided to buy and develop the estate that lay between the town and the sea. His name was John Corbett, and confusingly the previous owners were called Corbet. However this simplified matters for the landlord of Tywyn's principal hostelry, the Corbet Arms, who was able to keep up with events by adding another 't'.

John Corbett built a sea-wall esplanade and a road called Marine Terrace, and the townsfolk acquired an unexpected sea view. In later years Tywyn became better known as the terminus for the Talyllyn mountain railway. But throughout all these changes the parish church of St Cadfan's continued to guard the town's great historical treasure, a pillar of stone with a Welsh inscription dating possibly from the seventh century.

The pillar was not always treated with such respect. At one time a local farmer used it as a gatepost, and it could still be mistaken for one, were it not for the inscription. It means in English: 'The body of Cingen lies beneath'. It may not be the most effusive of tributes, and of course it no longer applies, but wherever Cingen is resting he may be gratified to know that his epitaph has survived for nearly 1400 years.

We do know where Llewellyn the Great lies, and his carved stone coffin still looks as magnificent, though admittedly it is only half the age of Cingen's stone. It lies in a chapel in another Gwynedd town, **Llanrwst**. Prince Llewellyn, redoubtable opponent of the English invaders in the thirteenth century, was originally buried at the Abbey of Conway, but the body had to be removed to Llanrwst when Henry VIII dissolved the monasteries. This indignity inflicted by an English monarch has perhaps been redeemed by our present Queen, who revived his other title to confer it on her brother-in-law. Prince Llewellyn was also Lord of Snowdon.

The English of course had their own stone tombs and monuments, but they went in for brasses too. Most of them are reasonably modest affairs, but St Margaret's church, **King's Lynn** has the dubious distinction of claiming the two biggest brasses in Britain. One is a life-size figure of Adam de Walsoken with his wife, surrounded by angels, apostles, apple gatherers, corn merchants, and what is believed to be the earliest illustration of a post windmill. The brass is dated 1349, it is nearly 10 feet long and 6 feet wide and contains at least a hundred figures. The other is in memory of Robert

The earliest epitaph in Wales is at Tywyn parish church (top); it just says, in Welsh, 'The Body of Cingen lies beneath'. The body of Prince Llewellyn the Great lay in the stone coffin which was moved from Conwy to Llanrwst (above and right), but any epitaph has been lost.

Braunche, dated 1364. It is a foot shorter, but Robert scores an extra point over Mr de Walsoken by having two wives beside him. He also has an illustration of the Peacock Feast, the traditional King's Lynn welcome for visiting kings, given by the Mayor. Mr Braunche happened to hold that office when King Edward came to town, and he was determined that no one shall forget it. There are the servants bearing the peacocks, the musicians, the guests, even the cutlery and glasses on the table. The Feast gets as much prominence on the Braunche brass as most churches would give to the Last Supper.

Every picture on a monument, in brass or stone, tells some sort of story, often of more lasting interest than roast peacock. For instance, one can find a dramatic tale of passion, bigamy and repentance in **Wigan**, not usually associated with such wild goings-on. Sir Walter Bradshaigh lies cross-legged in the parish church, wearing his armour and looking depressed. And well he might, because he came home from the wars to find his wife Mabel had got tired of waiting and married again. It is said that as a penance she walked barefoot once a week for a year from Haigh Hall to Wigan Cross, which is still known as Mabs' cross. She is depicted at one end of the tomb kneeling beneath the cross, and at the other end, two knights are fighting. Whatever the outcome, all seems to have ended happily, since a second effigy of Mabel lies peacefully beside her husband.

Another lady with two loves in her life is depicted in St Mary's church, **Kidderminster**, but in her case it was all above board, since her first husband died before she married the second. However the brass portrays them as if they were a threesome; Sir Walter Cokesey on one side, Sir John Phelip who succeeded him on the other, and their wife Matilda in between. Both husbands are armed with swords and daggers, and from their expressions each one looks ready to use them if the other makes a move towards Matilda.

Kidderminster also has a much more attractive and elaborate memorial, erected 500 years later to the memory of

Sir Walter Bradshaigh looks ready to do battle as he lies in Wigan parish church, and small wonder: his wife Mabel had grown tired of waiting for his return from the wars and married again.

Panoramic memorials. Parishioners in Kidderminster were portrayed in all their various occupations in the memorial to their vicar, Lawrence Banks Sladen, the screen in their parish church (above and right). The war memorial at Bury, Lancashire, showed workers on the Home Front as well as the armed forces (far right).

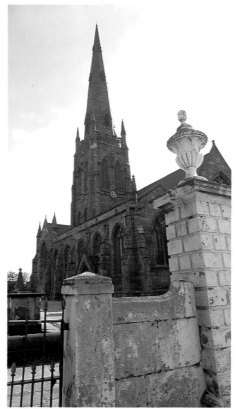

Lawrence Banks Sladen, who was vicar for 36 years. A varied assortment of his parishioners' activities are represented on a carved screen in the sanctuary: ploughing, mining, sheep-shearing, and of course, being Kidderminster, carpet making. There is also a plumber, apparently wearing pyjamas – it may have been an emergency call.

This panoramic style of commemorative carving was adopted at **Bury** in Lancashire for their First World War memorial. It is in the form of two bronze panels in the churchyard wall, one depicting members of the armed forces, the other with factory workers, fishermen, miners, a bus conductor and a postman, representing the home front.

A memorial at **Framlingham** church in Suffolk tells its story more subtly. In fact at a casual glance the effigies on the respective tombs of the third Duke of Norfolk and his son look merely like two more knights lying on their backs in eternal meditation. It is the discreet little inscription on the duke's collar, and the coronet lying beside the head of his son, which tell the rather poignant tale of their different fates as condemned prisoners of Henry VIII.

First the good news. The duke was due to be executed, but the king died the night before the execution and the sentence was never carried out. Hence the grateful inscription on his collar:

By the Grace of God I am what I am.

Now the bad news. His son was also sentenced to death, but in his case the king died on the night after the date of the execution. The unfortunate fellow duly lost his head, and while the sculptor baulked at making his effigy headless he did indicate his fate by removing his coronet.

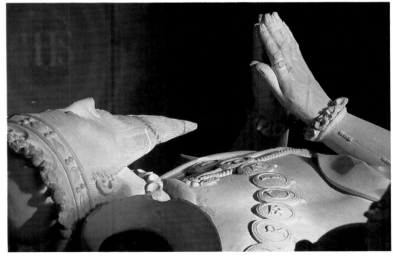

The third Duke of Norfolk and his son lie in Framlingham Church; one escaped execution by a happy chance, the other was unlucky. The story lies behind an inscription on a collar and a displaced coronet on their respective tombs.

The skull of Simon Tybald is preserved in the vestry of St Gregory's, Sudbury (above); the skull of Oliver Cromwell found a more appropriate resting place (far right).

The Earl of Shrewsbury left his heart in Whitchurch – under the porch of the parish church (above).

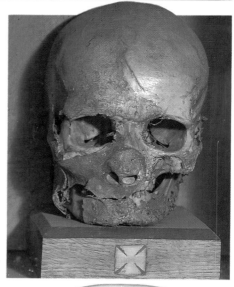

Near to this place was buried on 25 March 1960 the head of OLIVER CROMWELL Lord Protector of the Commonwealth of England, Scotland & Ireland, Fellow Commoner of this College 1616-7

Not far away in **Sudbury** they treated such situations with rather less delicacy. St Gregory's church has a reminder of another beheading. It is not just a displaced coronet but the actual head of Simon Tybald, who somehow managed to combine the offices of Archbishop of Canterbury and Chancellor of the Exchequer – an arrangement the present government has not yet thought of, but can it only be a matter of time?

The Archbishop–Chancellor was summarily executed by Wat Tyler's rebels during the Peasants' Revolt of 1381. In his fiscal capacity he had imposed that earlier poll tax, which provoked even greater wrath than the current one. He also urged Richard II to deal with the 'barefooted rebels' with ruthless severity, which he duly did, but not before they had dealt with the Archbishop. His head was retrieved from the Tower of London, where the rebels had detached it, and taken back to St Gregory's which he had rebuilt in earlier and happier days when he was only Bishop Simon of Sudbury. The vestry still houses the skull of this most unpopular of Chancellors; as Archbishop he might have had an unblemished reputation, but the man with the axe could hardly be expected to distinguish between the two.

The embalmed head of Oliver Cromwell has found its way back to Sidney Sussex College in **Cambridge**, where he was a student. But it is not on display; it was buried discreetly in the ante-chapel in 1960, long after any passions over his activities had subsided – though it has to be said that in parts of East Anglia there are neighbouring villages which still bear a grudge against each other because they were on opposite sides in the Civil War . . .

As you enter the parish church of **Whitchurch** in Shropshire you may be stepping, not on the head but on the heart of the first Earl of Shrewsbury. It was buried at his own wish in a silver urn beneath a stone slab in the porch. The earl deserved every consideration. The game old chap was killed in 1453 while fighting in the English army against the French – at the age of 80! His heart must have been not only in the right place but in remarkably good working order.

Incidentally, the church has another notable feature, the silken coat of arms of the eighteenth-century Speaker of the House of Commons, Sir Thomas Hanmer.

It is a long way from Westminster to Whitchurch, but it so happened that one of Sir Thomas's descendants, the Rev. H. Hanmer, was Rector of Whitchurch in the 1920s, and may well have been instrumental in installing this family relic in the vestry.

A number of other churches possess limbs or other pieces of anatomy of former parishioners, in various quality and condition, but for sheer quantity you can hardly beat the Norman crypt of **Hythe** parish church in Kent. Some 2000 human skulls were discovered there, along with 8000 thigh bones – a curious combination, since either each body had four thighs or half of them had no heads. What they did establish, however, was that Hythe people were 3 inches shorter than the average Englishman. This perhaps made them particularly suitable for the small carriages on the Romney Hythe and Dymchurch Light Railway.

Instead of burying this gruesome hoard, some 600 skulls are still stored in the crypt, laid out on shelves like wine-bottles. Some glare directly at visitors, others have turned to the wall in understandable embarrassment.

Like rows of bottles in a wine-cellar, rows of skulls are set out in the crypt of Hythe Parish church.

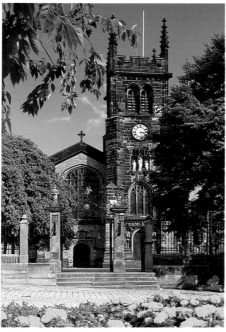

Impressive statistics. The Legh Pardon Brass at Macclesfield (above and left) records how the Legh family was pardoned for 26,000 years and 26 days. Mary Honywood of Coggeshall (right) had 367 descendants when she died. And Sarah Jarvis of Corsham (below) 'had fresh teeth some time before her death' at the age of 107.

Let us move to happier memorials. The church of St Michael and All Angels at **Macclesfield** has the Legh Pardon Brass, which records how Roger Legh was such a splendid fellow that he and his family were offered pardon by Pope St Gregory for 26,000 years and 26 days. The brass depicts the fortunate Mr Legh kneeling in gratitude before the Pope with his six grateful sons beside him. That was in 1506, so the Legh family must still be on good wicket for another 25,517 years – and of course 26 days.

The monument to Mary Honywood in **Coggeshall** Parish church, Essex, records another impressive statistic. She and her equally fertile offspring produced 367 descendants before she died. On the other hand Sarah Jarvis of **Corsham** in Wiltshire is remembered for quite a different achievement. She was 107 years old when she died in 1753 and her headstone notes that 'some time before her death she had fresh teeth'.

ERECTED·TO·THE·MEMORY·OF
VICTORIA·WOODHULL·MARTIN
AN·AMERICAN·CITIZEN
LONG·RESIDENT·IN·THIS·NEIGHBOURHOOD
WHO·DEVOTED·HERSELF·UNSPARINGLY·TO·ALL
THAT·COULD·PROMOTE·THE·GREAT·CAUSE·OF
ANGLO·AMERICAN·FRIENDSHIP
BORN·23ʳᵈ·SEPTEMBER·1838–DIED·9ᵗʰ·JUNE·1927

Victoria Woodhull Martin, who has a memorial in **Tewkesbury** Abbey, has the unique distinction of being the first woman to stand for the Presidency of the United States. She was born in Ohio, became a writer and lecturer on anything from feminism to finance, was elected to Congress, and in 1872 ran for President. Having failed to get elected, and having lost her second husband, she exchanged the hurly-burly of Washington politics for the peace and quiet of Tewkesbury, and in the words of her epitaph 'she devoted herself unsparingly to all that could promote the great cause of Anglo-American friendship'. She also gave a great deal of money to the Abbey, which may help to account for her rather grand memorial.

St Giles' church at **Wrexham** in Clwyd also has a notable American connection. It contains the tomb of Elihu Yale, whose parents emigrated from Wrexham in the seventeenth century. Elihu was born in Boston, and when the family returned to Wales 3 years later he must have retained a liking for foreign parts, because he went off and made a fortune as the East India Company's man in Madras. He must also have retained an affection for the country of his birth, because he became the benefactor of the university which bears his name.

General Richard Nicolls of **Ampthill** in Bedfordshire did not take such a bene-volent view of the New World. In 1664 he was ordered to drive the Dutch out of New Amsterdam and he duly did so, re-naming the town New York in honour of his patron, the Duke. However he was killed 8 years later in a naval battle, and the cannon-ball responsible for despatch-ing him is preserved on his monument at Ampthill.

Trans-Atlantic links. Victoria Woodhull Martin, buried in Tewkesbury (above, left) was the first woman to stand for President. Elihu Yale, buried in Wrexham (above) financed the university. General Richard Nicolls, buried in Ampthill (left and below) captured New Amsterdam and called it New York – then was killed by a cannon-ball, preserved on his monument.

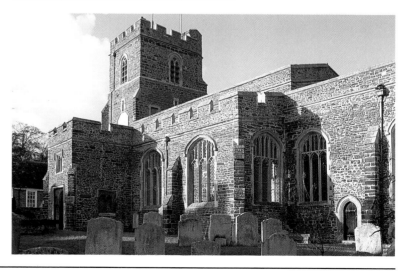

John Garmstone Hopkins of Worcester has his memory preserved by a photograph on his tomb (above); Benjamin Coldwell of Sheffield preferred to be remembered by the music of his favourite hymn (below).

The idea of adorning tombstones with items connected with the deceased was taken a step further by the family of 12-year-old John Garmstone Hopkins. He died in 1871 and was buried in the churchyard of St John's, Bedwardine, in **Worcester**. His memorial is one of the few in Britain, and certainly one of the earliest, to incorporate a photograph – though the practice is quite common in other countries. The lad's body dressed in a dark suit was photographed lying on a sofa draped with a shroud. The picture is on a glass base and its glass cover was sealed so effectively that it is still in near-perfect condition, though the surrounding stonework has decayed badly.

It is doubtful whether the church authorities would permit such an un-orthodox memorial these days, but it is interesting to discover what can still achieve approval. In the churchyard at **Chipping Norton** there is a tombstone in the shape of a five-barred gate, with an enormous horseshoe in the centre and a horse's head looking through it. It is in memory of Davey Barnard, who died as recently as 1973. On the top bar of the gate is the message from his wife Daisy:

Davey, I love you.

Benjamin Coldwell of **Sheffield** also had an unusual idea for his tombstone. It is engraved with, presumably, his favourite hymn – not merely the words but the notes of the music. The verse starts, perhaps appropriately, 'Great God! What do I see . . .'

And from the musical to the whimsical. John Hollings of **Stroud** in Gloucester-shire had a disagreement with someone who announced that he hoped to live long enough to see him 'safe under-ground'. Mr Hollings did in fact die before him, but he left orders that his coffin should not be buried, but be covered with a pile of stones, thus depriving his old

adversary of that pleasure. The stones are still piled in the churchyard, and John Hollings is probably still chuckling.

The grave-diggers at **Maldon** in Essex might have been grateful if Edward Bright had left the same instructions. When he died in 1750 he was reputed to be the biggest man in England, turning the scales at 44 stones. It was a major task to dig a grave big enough to accommodate him, and it is said that at the funeral a special crane had to be used to lower him into it.

Mr Bright was one of a long line of enormous men who have created this problem over the years, commencing perhaps with a fifth-century giant called Ewan Caesarius, who was buried next to St Andrew's church at **Penrith** in Cumbria. Ewan's precise statistics are not known, but the two stones which are said to mark the extremities of his grave are 15 feet apart . . .

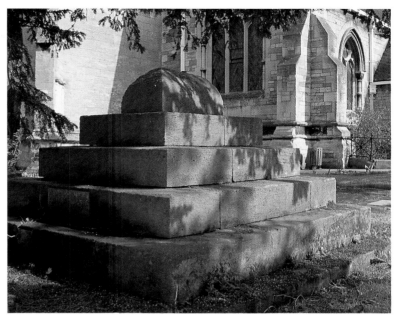

John Hollings was buried above ground at Stroud to thwart an enemy (above). Edward Bright was buried below ground, but with some difficulty, at Maldon (below). And judging by his grave Ewan Caesarius must have also presented a weighty problem at Penrith (far left).

Epitaph oddities. Sir Thomas Cockayne had the first one to rhyme (above), Robert Phillips wrote his own, a little sourly (below); but who wrote the accusation by Sarah Smith (bottom)?

The first rhyming epitaph which still exists is generally reckoned to be the laudatory verse written on the fifteenth-century tomb of Sir Thomas Cockayne in **Ashbourne** church, Derbyshire. Sir Thomas

was a knight so worshipfull,
so vertuous wise and pityfull,
his deeds deserve that his good name
live here in everlasting fame.

There's a lot more of the same.

Since then the epitaph writers have made full use of congratulatory couplets on tombstones, but some of their verses have a rather deeper significance. There is the bitter little verse, for instance, which Robert Philips wrote for his own epitaph in **Kingsbridge** church in Devon:

Here lie I at the chancel door,
here lie I because I'm poor.
The further in the more you'll pay,
here lie I as warm as they.

Much more macabre is the rhyme on Sarah Smith's tombstone at St Margaret's church, **Newcastle-under-Lyme**. When she died in 1763 her relatives used her epitaph to accuse her suspected murderer.

It was G–S B–W that brought me to my end,
dear parents mourn not for me
for God will stand my Friend.
With half a pint of Poyson
he came to visit me.
Write this on my grave
that all that read it may see.

By putting the words in Sarah's mouth did the writer evade the laws of libel? Or did G–S B–W really poison her, and as a result of that accusing tombstone met his just desserts? Either way, I doubt if you could get away with it today.

The story not of a murder but of the break-up of a marriage lies behind the simple inscription on the tomb of 5-year-old Penelope Boothby, in the same church as Sir Thomas Cockayne's at **Ashbourne**.

She was in form and intellect most
exquisite. The unfortunate parents
ventured their all on this frail bark,
and the wreck was total.

Total indeed. Sir Brooke and Dame Susannah Boothby had disagreed over their daughter's medical treatment, and after the funeral Dame Susannah left her husband at the grave side and never returned.

Penelope does have a happier memorial. Her portrait by Sir Joshua Reynolds, called 'Simplicity', is one of his most famous works. And if you think it looks very like Sir John Millais's much later portrait called 'Cherry Ripe', then full marks, because the girl Millais painted had dressed up for a party as Penelope, wearing a similar mob cap and dress.

Sometimes an epitaph is used to warn others not to risk a similar fate. In **Devizes** churchyard there is a memorial to five young people who were drowned in a pond in 1751. It is not the dangerous

Penelope Boothby's death (above, left) caused her parents to part at the graveside. The death of five young people at Devizes was used as a warning to others (above). And the death of a farmer at Darlington created Hell's Kettles (below).

nature of the pond which the epitaph warns of, but the fact that they died on the Sabbath, when they should have been at their devotions instead of frolicking around the countryside. The memorial was erected by public subscription 'as a solemn Monitor to young people to remember their Creator in the days of their youth'.

An unknown farmer of **Darlington** – in the days when Darlington had farms – also offended against the rules of the church, it is said, by taking his hay waggons and horses out to work on St Barnabas Day, an ecclesiastical day of rest. Retribution came not only to the farmer but to his waggons, his horses, and anyone who might have been hitching a ride. The whole lot was swallowed up in two deep pools which became known as Hell's Kettles. There is no memorial to the farmer, unless it be the pools, where his ghost may still be seen on St Barnabas Day, and his cries may still be heard . . .

Sir Henry Lee of Aylesbury not only built a monument for his wife and three children, he asked that a bunch of crimson flowers be always placed on it in their memory. Four centuries later there are still flowers on the memorial.

There is an implicit warning in the hot-air balloon which is depicted on the tombstone of Miss Lily Cove at **Haworth** church in Yorkshire. Miss Cove has been somewhat overshadowed by those other Haworth ladies, the Brontës, but she must have been a remarkable woman, because she made an ascent by balloon to test out a new parachute. Although it is the balloon which is featured on the tombstone, it should really be the parachute. It never opened.

The only warning implied by John Small's tombstone at **Petersfield** in Hampshire is not to become so obsessed by cricket that you are given the epitaph:

Bowled by death's unerring ball.

Who could rest easy under that! Mark Sharp, an eighteenth-century carpenter, preferred to be remembered by the tools of his trade, and they are all carved on his tombstone at **Lewes** in Sussex – a plane, a saw, a hammer and chisel, the entire tool-kit. The stonemason ran out of space before he got around to adding Mr Sharp's name; he had to make do with initials.

Finally Sir Henry Lee had a more thoughtful way of preserving the memory of his wife and three children. They have a monument in St Mary's church, **Aylesbury**, dated 1584. An inscription asks that a bunch of crimson flowers be placed on the memorial.

That kind of request would not have appealed to the writer Edna St Vincent Millay, who composed for her own epitaph the instructions:

Heap not on this mount,
roses that she loved so well.
Why bewilder her with roses,
that she cannot see or smell?

But the good parishioners of Aylesbury obviously do not share her rather jaundiced view. Four centuries after the demise of Lady Lee and her children, they still place crimson flowers on their memorial.

STILL NO JERUSALEM – BUT THE MILLS AREN'T ALL BAD

The Industrial Revolution did a great deal for the prosperity of Britain; it did nothing at all for the beauty of our towns. The mills may not all have been dark, and very few were actually Satanic, but most of them were exceedingly ugly, and those that remain have not exactly mellowed with age. But some at least have character, and one or two have unexpected touches of whimsy. The coming of the railways, on the other hand, produced some magnificent architectural fantasies. I have quoted Auden's description of cathedrals: 'luxury liners laden with souls'. Some of our great railway stations could equally be cathedrals with congregations of commuters . . .

Derby had the first silk mill in England (above) – not quite an architectural gem, but the gates look nice. The stockingers' cottages at Stapleford (below) and the weaving works at Coventry (right) had workroom windows above, not-so-bright living quarters below.

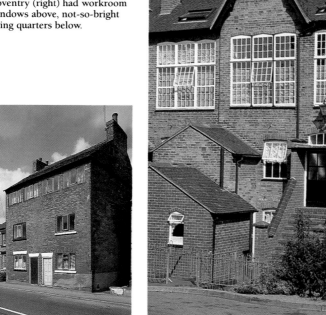

Even before young James Watt was inspired by a steaming kettle and effectively launched the Industrial Revolution, there was a fair amount of industry in some of our towns, albeit without the benefit of steam power. For instance, when you think of **Derby** you may think of Rolls-Royce, or Royal Crown Derby, or the engineering works of the old Midland Railway. But even in Norman times it had fourteen flour mills, it later produced cloth, beer and soap, and in 1717 it created industrial history with the first silk mill in England. The mill looks as dour a building as those which followed it, but they have smartened it up with a splendid wrought-iron gate picked out in gold, said to be one of the finest examples of that kind of work in Britain.

Not far away at **Stapleford** in Nottinghamshire is another building to remind us of the earlier days of mass-produced clothing. It is a row of cottages with almost the entire top floors given over to windows. These were stockingers' cottages, designed to provide the maximum light for the womenfolk operating their framework knitting machines.

Joseph Cash also believed in the top-floor theory of industrial production. When he built his weaving works in **Coventry** the living quarters were downstairs and the looms were above. His workers commuted to work vertically through trapdoors in the ceilings. It must have been a tedious existence, since their work had got on top of them, permanently. The workshops are now used as store-rooms, but those labels which every schoolchild was supposed to have on socks and jackets are still made on the same site.

Cloth was produced in towns and cities across the breadth of Britain, from Norwich in the east, thanks to the Dutch weavers and their skill with worsted, to places like **Trowbridge** in the west. 'Trowbridge flourishith by drapery', said a man with a lisp called Leland in the sixteenth century, and the flourishithing continues today, with a number of mills still in action. At Studley Mills they still have the building called the handle house, where they stored the teasels which were used to raise a nap on the cloth. The teasels needed a through-flow of air to dry them, and the architect provided this in very simple fashion by building walls with lots of holes in. In fact he left out every other brick in every other row; somehow the wall stayed up.

Trowbridge has another reminder of the early days of industrialisation. In the churchyard there is a monument to Thomas Helliker, who objected so strongly to the newfangled powerloom that he led a riot against the mill owners. Like similar riots at Peterloo and elsewhere, it failed to halt the march of the machines, and Helliker was executed in 1803. He was just 19.

Another kind of mill which preceded the days of steam is still preserved at **Faversham** in Kent. Faversham may seem the most peaceful of country towns, with its fine old Tudor and Stuart houses – Abbey Street alone has fifty listed buildings – but until as recently as the 1930s it was the centre of Britain's explosives industry. Much of its prosperity came from the manufacture of gunpowder.

The gunpowder mills, powered by water and claimed to be the oldest of their type in the world, stretched for the best part of a mile from Faversham Creek to Ospringe. They needed all that space because, very wisely, they were built at considerable distances from one another, with trees planted in between, and they were also quite flimsily constructed. This meant that if one of them exploded, it did not blow up all the rest. The flimsiness also meant that there was not a lot of protection for anyone inside the exploding mill or in the immediate vicinity. One of the mills where they used to mix the saltpetre with the sulphur has been restored, to a rather higher safety standard than when it was built in the 1760s.

A less hazardous product – you could only prick your finger – came out of another water-powered mill at **Redditch** in Hereford and Worcester. Forge Mill was built in the early eighteenth century for needle-scouring. In those days needle-making was a major local industry, introduced by the monks at a long-vanished abbey. Much of the industry has

Perforated walls to provide plenty of air to dry the teasels at Studley Mills in Trowbridge (left). Well spaced out buildings to provide plenty of protection at the gunpowder mills at Faversham (below).

The needle-scouring mill at Redditch (above) is still given a whirl once a week for the tourists. Newcomen's steam engine at Dartmouth is still capable of pumping out a mine if required (right).

vanished too, with the transformation of Old Redditch into Redditch New Town, but the needle-scouring mill continued to operate commercially until the 1960s. It is now given a nostalgic whirl once a week for the tourists.

While James Watt gets most of the glory for inventing the steam engine, the first chap to produce one was Thomas Newcomen, before James was born. Indeed it was only when young Watt was asked to repair a model of a Newcomen engine, owned by the University of Glasgow where he worked, that he became absorbed in making it more efficient. But though these engines wasted a lot of the energy they produced, they were still powerful enough to pump water out of deep coal mines, and one of them has been erected in the Royal Avenue Gardens at **Dartmouth** in Newcomen's honour.

Dartmouth may seem a long way from the major coalfields but this was Newcomen's home town; he had an ironmongery business there at the end of the seventeenth century, and built his first engine in 1712. The one in Royal Avenue Gardens is still in working order, and Dartmouth likes to think it is the oldest atmospheric steam engine still capable, if necessary, of pumping out a flooded mine.

While they laud Newcomen's memory in Dartmouth, how much more grateful they must have been in places like **Blyth** in Northumberland, one of the main ports for the North of England coalfields, which owed its existence to the successful operations of the mining industry. The old wooden chutes where the coal was poured into the ships' holds stand on the river bank, and there is still one of the old stable blocks for the colliery horses. Sadly it has been allowed to deteriorate, but the rusting iron tracery in the windows can just be made out, though the windows themselves are all broken. Inside there are stalls for sixteen horses, and an outside staircase leads to the hayloft above.

Perhaps the citizens of Blyth have little interest in such crumbling relics because they preserve the memory of the coal-mining days in a rather more attractive way. A local team of dancers performs the 'rapper', which looks rather like a sword dance – indeed the performers are the Royal Earsdon Sword Dancers – but the rappers were sticks used in the mines, and the dancers dress like Victorian miners of a century or more ago.

Another great northern coal port was **Whitehaven** in Cumbria, where they have some of the oldest coaling wharves in Britain. Work on the Old Quay was started in 1634, 30 years before Newcomen was born, and coal was shipped from local pits all over the country. In the eighteenth century the principal mine owner was the first Earl of Lonsdale, a man with a taste for turrets. He not only built Whitehaven Castle, now a hospital, but made all the mine buildings look like castles too. Most of them are derelict or demolished, but the fan house of one pit still stands, its battlemented walls looking more suitable for boiling oil than cooling coal. It is preserved as a memorial to over a hundred miners who were killed in an underground explosion. The entrance lodge to one of the pits was used as a cafe until a couple of years ago, when it had to be abandoned because the cliff was unsafe.

Mining reminders in the north. Colliery horses used to be stabled in these stalls at Blyth (above). Miners used to work beneath castle-like battlements at Whitehaven (below).

Whitehaven also has that symbol of the Industrial Revolution, a tall chimney – in this case not to carry away smoke but to bring air into the mine. But it was no ordinary chimney. Lord Lonsdale not only enjoyed a good turret, he had a thing about candlesticks. It is said that when he was asked if he had any thoughts about the design of the chimney he indicated a candlestick and said, 'Build it like that'. Thus the town acquired what is always known locally as the Candlestick Chimney. It would have been interesting if his lordship had preferred organ pipes or broomsticks . . .

Industrial chimneys do seem to bring out the eccentric in mine owners and mill masters. The old tweed mill at **Chipping Norton**, for example, is completely dominated by its single chimney, which sticks out of the middle of the building from a central dome like a candle in the middle of a cake. The mill is now a block of flats, but nobody had the heart to remove this monstrous projection. The residents can at least have the tallest television aerial in Gloucestershire . . .

The most ornate factory chimney in Britain must surely be Wainhouse Tower in **Halifax**, which was intended to serve the adjoining dyeworks but was never connected. John Wainhouse sold the dyeworks and the new owner did not fancy buying the chimney as well. It was certainly something of an extravagance; Mr Wainwright equipped it with a spiral staircase leading to a balcony 250 feet above the ground, and there was an elegant cupola on top of that. It is questionable whether the smoke would ever have found its way out.

Mr Wainhouse did not have a lot of luck with that chimney. Not only did he fail to sell it, but when he climbed up it he found the balcony parapet was so high he couldn't see the view . . .

Chimney curiosities. Lord Lonsdale wanted a ventilation shaft in Whitehaven that looked like a candlestick (left); John Wainhouse wanted a dyeworks chimney with an observation balcony (far left) in Halifax.

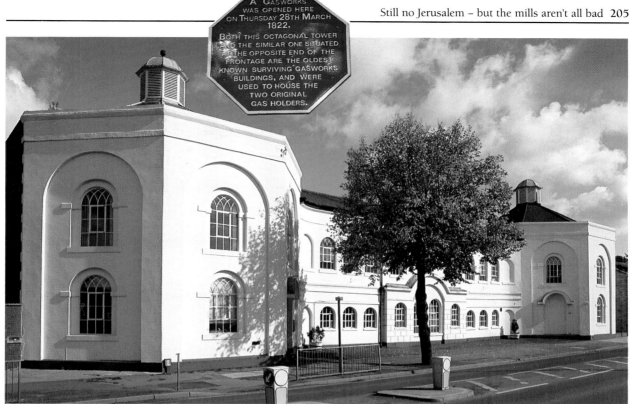

A GASWORKS WAS OPENED HERE ON THURSDAY 28TH MARCH 1822. BOTH THIS OCTAGONAL TOWER AND THE SIMILAR ONE SITUATED AT THE OPPOSITE END OF THE FRONTAGE ARE THE OLDEST KNOWN SURVIVING GASWORKS BUILDINGS, AND WERE USED TO HOUSE THE TWO ORIGINAL GAS HOLDERS.

Chimneys dominated the industrial skyline during the age of coal and steam, but then came a new source of power, gas, and a new blot on the landscape, the gasholder. It is not easy to make an ugly gasholder look anything else but an ugly gasholder; full marks therefore to the ingenious gasmen of **Warwick** who made theirs look like a Regency mansion. The two holders were encased in octagonal towers with fake windows and jolly little cupolas on the roof. They were built in 1822 and are claimed to be England's oldest.

Down in Cornwall, however, William Murdock was well ahead of Warwick in creating his own personal gas supply. He set up his own gas retorts in **Redruth** in 1792, and his house behind Druid's Hall is said to be the first private house fitted with gas lighting.

Now that gas is piped from the North Sea many towns have found their gasworks redundant. Inevitably, as they have started to disappear, they have come to be regarded with affectionate nostalgia instead of very natural distaste. At **Fakenham**

The oldest gasworks in England, made to look like a country mansion at Warwick (above). And the first house to be equipped with gas lighting, looking like any other house at Redruth (left).

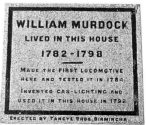

WILLIAM MURDOCK LIVED IN THIS HOUSE 1782-1798

MADE THE FIRST LOCOMOTIVE HERE AND TESTED IT IN 1784

INVENTED GAS-LIGHTING AND USED IT IN THIS HOUSE IN 1792

ERECTED BY TANGYE BROS, BIRMINGHAM

Names that have lived on, one way or another. The Yorkshire Penny Bank has moved on a long way from pennies, but the wrought iron inscription over the door in Bradford remains. Pryce Jones founded the mail order industry in his warehouse in Newtown; it has expanded somewhat since then, but the name of 'Jones the Catalogue' remains on the roof (far right).

in Norfolk they lovingly preserve the rather seedy retort house and the barrows and shovels used by the stokers – much to the amazement of the surviving stokers, who spent their working life getting hot and filthy stoking those boilers and cannot imagine why anyone would want to preserve the place.

Nevertheless Fakenham has turned its old gasworks into the only museum of its kind in England. There is another at Biggar in Scotland, but I am assured that Biggar is in fact smaller. They also claim that the retorts and the pipes that lead from them to the gasholder and the tarpit are the last of their kind. There has been much cleaning and polishing, and what was regarded thirty years ago as something of an eyesore received the final accolade of approval when the restored gasworks was officially opened to the public by the Duke of Gloucester. He must treasure that entry in his engagement diary: '3 pm Open gasworks' . . .

Alongside the great industrial developments of the last century there grew up the financial services to handle the massive profits made by the owners, and the modest wages earned by their employees. Most of these employees had problems enough just surviving, let alone saving,

but the Penny Bank was invented to coax their pennies from them. In **Bradford** the Penny Bank has long been absorbed by the Yorkshire Bank, but its name lives on in the wrought-iron inscription on the façade.

Pryce Jones had a different idea for putting the workers' pennies to good use. He was involved in the manufacture of Welsh flannel in **Newtown**, Powys, and owned the Royal Welsh Warehouse near the railway station. It turned out to be a very convenient site when he started offering his wares for sale by post in 1859. He is credited – if credit is the word – with being the founder of the mail order industry. When the next heap of junk mail lands on your doormat, you may care to cast a kindly thought in the direction of Newtown and the memory of Jones the Catalogue.

Newtown was also the home of Robert Owen, who created another commercial first. He was a dedicated opponent of the capitalist system, long before Marx had the same idea, and he campaigned for industry to be controlled by the workers. He conducted his personal industrial revolution on both sides of the Atlantic, and just as Pryce Jones could claim to have founded the mail order business, Robert Owen could claim to have founded the co-operative movement. Certainly his fellow townsfolk hold him in greater esteem. They have put up a statue and created a museum in Owen's

memory; Pryce Jones has just got a name board on top of his old warehouse.

In the twentieth century industrial architects have shown rather more imagination than their Victorian predecessors. For instance, the Bata shoe factory at **Tilbury** in Essex was built in the 1930s in the same style as the parent factory, thus bringing a Czechoslovakian flavour to this ancient English port. Or there is the Willis, Faber and Dumas building in **Ipswich**, the most unusual feature of which is only visible from the air – its roof is covered in grass. But for really remarkable variations on a simple basic theme one cannot beat our British railway stations.

The Bata factory brought a touch of Czechoslovakia to Tilbury (below).

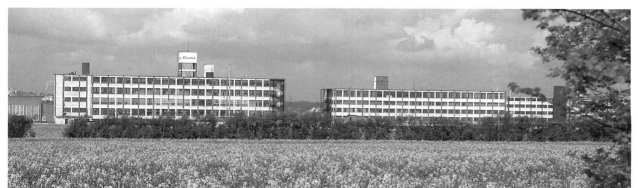

The Willis, Faber and Dumas building brought a touch of high-rise lawn-mowing to Ipswich.

Ideas above their station. Assorted railway architecture at the Curzon Street goods station in Birmingham (above), the citadel station, Carlisle (right) and the central station at Huddersfield (below).

British airports are built for much the same purpose, the transporting of passengers, but every airport looks alike, give or take the length of the queues. Nobody puts a Greek portico over the entrance or Doric pillars in the departure lounge. Yet railway stations seem to cover every architectural period and style, whether it be the Jacobean façade at Stoke-on-Trent, or the heraldic coats of arms and shields at **Carlisle**, or the Corinthian portico at **Huddersfield**, which makes the station look like a city hall, except that instead of the town's coat of arms there is the British Rail insignia over the portal.

Greek Revival seems to be the favourite. The old Monkwearmouth station in **Sunderland**, now appropriately a museum, is a good example; the Curzon Street goods station in **Birmingham**, with its 50-foot Ionic columns, is another.

Brunel's train shed at Temple Meads station in **Bristol**, with its mock hammer-beam roof, is probably the most famous

example of elaborate station architecture – not counting St Pancras, which comes under the heading of fairy castles. Since it became redundant the train shed has been a museum and an exhibition hall. People have played squash in it and parked cars in it. Its greatest moment of glory was when it became a venue for TV's *Antiques Road Show* . . .

My favourite station, however, is **Great Malvern**, which was actually built by the Victorians to look like a Victorian station, quite a rare display of restraint. They ornamented its iron pillars with brightly painted floral decorations, which give a very pleasant vista along the platforms; and they put a big old station clock just where it was needed – slap in the middle.

Brunel may have designed Britain's most impressive train shed at Bristol Temple Meads (above), but Great Malvern's station pillars are prettier (below).

Liverpool Road station in Manchester, the first to be purpose-built for passengers, is now a Grade One listed building (above). The Howard Street warehouse in Shrewsbury, originally a butter market, has survived its experience under British Rail and is now an entertainments centre (below).

Although the North Road station in Darlington makes great play of the fact that this was where the first public railway opened in 1825, the first custom-built passenger station was not completed for another five years – and not in Darlington. Liverpool Road station in **Manchester** is the oldest railway station in the world; it was the first to be built for the transporting of passengers and goods in steam-hauled trains. It was opened by the Duke of Wellington, who despatched the first train to Liverpool. Later it was used only for goods traffic; it is now a Grade One listed building.

Finally a building in **Shrewsbury** which served the railway for many years as a warehouse for freight traffic, though it was originally built as a butter market for produce arriving on the Shropshire

Union Canal. The Howard Street warehouse, as it came to be known, is a rare example of good nineteenth-century industrial architecture which has somehow survived through changing fortunes and uses, and has now come into its own again.

It was built in 1835 with a brick vaulted cellar for storage and an upper floor for the butter market. The outside was on classical lines, but inside it had cast-iron columns and an open truss roof. After the railway took it over, part of the front façade was moved 6 feet back – not so much a face-lift as a face-push. The building continued to receive scant respect; thieves stole most of the lead off the roof, it fell into decay, and British Rail decided to get rid of it. The neighbouring Post Office proposed knocking it down to make a car park.

The local preservation societies, which seem to have taken little notice of it before, now sprang to its defence. So did Her Majesty's Inspectors. They said it should be preserved if it could be put to some community use, and this indeed is what has happened. It has become an arts and entertainments centre, with the cellars converted into a bar, a dance hall and restaurant in the main warehouse, and instead of a weighbridge, a Wurlitzer organ.

Here at least, the Industrial Revolution has come full circle.

SOME DAY
MY PLINTH
WILL COME

'The erection of a monument is superfluous; our memory will endure if our lives have deserved it.' So said Pliny the Younger, which presumably meant no plinth for poor old Pliny the Elder. Nevertheless in the 1900 years that have passed since then, we have spent much of our time erecting monuments in towns all over Britain, most of which look monumentally boring. But sometimes they can mark an event which is unusual enough to be worth remembering, and here and there among the dreary dignitaries and the noble nonentities there are actually some quite interesting people . . .

Queen Victoria was not amused by a German bomber (above). Cromwell seemed rarely amused by anything (above, right) but he does look a little more relaxed at his weekend retreat (opposite).

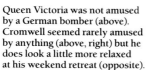

A German bomb moved this statue one inch on its plinth on the 14th. November 1940

Monarchs have always been popular subjects for statues, more than even their most popular subjects, and as Queen Victoria was monarch the longest, and had the most time to tour her domain, she has more statues scattered about than most. They all look much the same – Anna Neagle in a bun and long frock – and the statue at **Leamington Spa** is no exception, but this regal figure did have a most unregal experience. On 14th November 1940, a German pilot had the temerity to deposit a bomb close enough to Queen Victoria to move her one inch, an indignity which, judging by her expression, offended her deeply. In fact she grasps the orb as though it were a hand grenade, ready to hurl it at the wretched fellow if he ever dares to return.

Oliver Cromwell was also high in the statue league table, and is generally portrayed as an even sterner figure than Victoria. Nowhere does he look grimmer than beside the bridge at **Warrington** in Lancashire, clad in full battle gear and armed with sword and Bible. The statue commemorates his entry into the town just after he had won a famous victory at Preston, but apparently it took more than a famous victory to cheer him up.

James Starley is honoured in Coventry for inventing bicycles – but he invented an adjustable candlestick and a one-stringed window blind too.

He does look slightly less formidable, however, at **St Ives** in Cambridgeshire, where he acquired one of his numerous country properties and did a spot of farming on his weekends off. The locals were perhaps more accustomed to seeing him prodding a pig than severing a head or saving a soul, and his statue depicts him in more relaxed mood with a rather imposing, almost rakish hat instead of his customary helmet. The fancy hat was perhaps the Cromwellian equivalent of green wellies . . .

If a sculptor wanted to make his subject look particularly imposing, he put him on a horse. This must have come quite expensive, since a horse involves a lot more sculpting than a human, but we do have a fair number of mounted monarchs and horsy heroes perched in our town squares. How much rarer to find a statue which features not a horse, but a bike. The monument in **Coventry** to James Starley boasts not just one bicycle, but two tricycles – the Coventry Rotary and the Royal Salvo. Both of them were invented by Mr Starley, along with the Ariel Safety cycle, various other trikes and even a quadricycle.

Not content with that, he also devised an adjustable candlestick, a one-stringed window blind and a sewing machine, but only his cycles really caught on. They made Coventry the centre of the cycle manufacturing industry, and this is duly recognised by his monument. He is not actually riding a cycle, nor indeed is it his statue which appears above them, but a portrayal of Fame. His own presence is only indicated by a medallion portrait.

James Starley is honoured in Coventry for inventing bicycles – but he invented an adjustable candlestick and a one-stringed window blind too.

John English's party trick in Whickham was to smash holes in the ceiling with his head (above and right). Samuel Johnson, on the other hand, used his head to better purpose. But at Uttoxeter he is remembered, not for his learning, but for his drenching; it was a penance for a childhood misdemeanour (far right).

But by the time it was erected he was in no position to argue; he had already been dead for 3 years.

John English, on the other hand, had the privilege of seeing a bust erected in his memory while he was still alive. He arrived at **Whickham**, in Tyne and Wear, in the 1830s to work as a mason on the Scotswood suspension bridge, and apparently endeared himself to the locals by giving displays of strength. He stood nearly 6½ feet tall and was known as Lang Jack; his party piece at Saturday

night hops was to jump in the air and smash a hole in the ceiling with his head.

It was obviously inadvisable to offend Lang Jack. It is said that when his dog was run over by a waggon he picked up the waggon and turned it on its side, along with the horse that was pulling it. As it was full of stones from the local quarry at the time, this was quite a feat. As a stone-mason himself he no doubt took a professional interest in the sculpting of his bust, which was done by a man called John Norvell. Mr Norvell must have found it a nerve-wracking assignment, particularly if he had seen the incident with the waggon, but fortunately Lang Jack seems to have approved and he lived to sculpt another day.

Great thinkers are usually portrayed doing a bit of great thinking, so it is refreshing to find the illustrious Dr Samuel Johnson remembered in **Uttoxeter** in much more humble fashion. A sculpture in the Market Place shows him as an old man standing bareheaded and miserable in the rain. This was how he did penance for a childhood misdemeanour which had obviously preyed

on his mind for the rest of his life. His father was a bookseller in Lichfield and also ran a stall in Uttoxeter market. He asked his son to give him a hand on the stall, but young Samuel was too proud to do so.

In his seventies he returned to the spot where his father's stall used to stand, and remained there bareheaded in the rain for several hours. Passers-by probably thought he was quite potty, and indeed may have said so, because he took the trouble to explain afterwards: 'In contrition I stood, and I hope the penance was expiatory.' That is how his words are recorded, though after such a soaking, what sounded like 'contrition' might really have been 'atishoo'.

There may seem nothing unusual about the statue of Josiah Wedgwood at **Stoke-on-Trent**. He stands in the middle of Winton Square, appropriately with his back to the pub, since he greatly disapproved of such places – the jug he holds is not for refreshment, but merely to demonstrate his products. What must have surprised those who knew him, though, is that he is standing on two good

legs. In fact he lost a leg through illness at quite an early age, certainly before he achieved his fame. Did he have a remarkably lifelike artificial limb? Is the statue just an idealistic portrayal? Or did nobody bother to tell the sculptor?

No doubt at all about the unusual appearance of Dr William Price's statue at **Llantrisant** in Mid-Glamorgan. Llantrisant is best known in England as the home of the Royal Mint – when I went there with *Any Questions?* I was urged by a bored colleague to introduce this otherwise unremarkable town as 'the hole with the Mint in it'. But among the Welsh it is Dr Price who first put Llantrisant on the map.

The statue of Dr William Price in Llantrisant (below), a man with mysterious headgear. And the statue of Josiah Wedgwood in Stoke-on-Trent (below, left), a man with a mysterious leg.

Sir Thomas Browne, the Norwich doctor who yearned for an urn. He was an advocate of cremation, arguing that bones could be 'gnaw'd out of their grave'. But he was buried nevertheless, and many years later his bones were indeed 'gnaw'd out' by workmen digging another grave. His skull was removed and had various adventures before being returned to his tomb and an un-urned rest.

He was born there in 1800 and became an ardent advocate of vegetarianism, nudism and free love, none of which went down terribly well in nineteenth-century Wales. He wore a foxskin head-dress, faithfully reproduced on the statue, and he lived according to the teachings of the Druids. But his most significant hobby-horse, and one which he rode so determinedly that it had a permanent impact on the laws of Britain, was cremation. His son died in infancy (though not before he had been christened, with Dr Price's usual flair for the unorthodox, Iesu-Crist) and his father attempted to cremate the body on Llantrisant Common. The outraged locals took him to court, but he was declared innocent of any crime, and as a result of the ruling, cremation became recognised as a legal procedure.

How that would have delighted an earlier doctor whose statue is on Hay Hill in **Norwich**. Sir Thomas Browne was born nearly two centuries before Dr Price, but he too was in favour of cremation. He is best known for his medical treatises, but outside medicine his main interests were ornithology – he kept a tame bittern in his back garden – and the Roman practice of burning the bodies of the deceased. He wrote a book about the advantages of not burying bones to be 'gnaw'd out of their grave'; indeed the statue depicts him gazing hopefully at a burial urn.

Alas, his hopes were not realised – and his worst fears were. He was buried in the sanctuary of St Peter Mancroft, and sure enough his bones were 'gnaw'd out' many years later by workmen digging another grave. His skull was removed and after

various adventures put on show at the Norfolk and Norwich Hospital, until some kindly soul took pity on the hapless Sir Thomas and returned it to his tomb in 1922. No wonder his statue gazes with such yearning at that urn.

Another statue to an East Anglian doctor also features an object of affection. In fact, that is all it does feature. In **Aldeburgh** there is the statue of a terrier, erected not in memory of the dog but of his master. The inscription explains that it was 'erected by the people of the borough to Dr Robin P. M. Acheson, who cared for them 1931-1959'.

Many famous sailors have statues and monuments in their memory – and I'll be coming to good old Horatio in a moment. But I have a special soft spot for George Smith, a trawler skipper whose statue stands on the Boulevard in **Hull**.

Skipper Smith was going about his business in October 1904, fishing off the Dogger Bank, when he and his fellow trawlermen had the singular misfortune to be taken for Japanese torpedo boats by the Imperial Russian Navy. Why they should have thought the Japanese were on manoeuvres off the Dogger Bank I cannot explain, but they let fly with their heavy guns and without much difficulty sank a considerable proportion of the Hull fishing fleet.

Miraculously there were only two fatalities, one of whom was George Smith. His statue depicts him holding up one hand, as if vainly trying to ward off the Russian Navy. It could have been of little consolation to him that the Russians eventually met the real Japanese fleet, and were ignominiously defeated.

The statue of a terrier at Aldeburgh (above, left) is a reminder of a much-loved doctor. The statue of Skipper Smith at Hull (above) is a reminder of a much-confused Russian admiral.

Lord Hill on his monument in Shrewsbury (above) and Britannia on Nelson's column in Great Yarmouth (above, right). George IV should have been on top of the Naval Column at Devonport, but the money ran out.

Now for Horatio. Nelson's Column in Trafalgar Square is the one that gets all the publicity, but there is another Nelson's Column, somewhat shorter, in his native county of Norfolk. It stands on the front at **Great Yarmouth**, surmounted not by that familiar figure in admiral's uniform with eyepatch and empty sleeve, but by Britannia. She faces inland instead of out to sea, as one might expect. Perhaps she is trying to catch a glimpse of another memorial to him, which stands by his old grammar school in Norwich.

Incidentally Nelson did not have a monopoly of very high columns. One of the Duke of Wellington's commanders, Lord Hill, has one in **Shrewsbury** which is only 11 feet shorter than the column in Trafalgar Square, and the Naval Column at **Devonport**, erected to mark the renaming of Plymouth Dock in 1824, is only 9 feet shorter than that. The story goes that it should have been rather higher, since it was supposed to have a statue of George IV on top – but the money ran out. The **Plymouth** authorities fared rather better with their more famous column, the Armada Memorial; they did manage to put a figure on top of that, but like Great Yarmouth, all they could think of was Britannia.

The stone pyramid which stands in Grove Place, **Falmouth**, has no figure on it at all, nor indeed is there any explanation of who erected it, or why, or when. The plaque merely says it commemorates 'the last of the Killigrew family'. It is popularly regarded, however, as commemorating all the Killigrews, a remarkable clan who combined philanthropy with piracy and, one way or another, laid the foundations of Falmouth's prosperity. The family history reads like a Poldark novel; let me give you a flavour.

John Killigrew was the first governor of Pendennis Castle, but he went in for piracy on the side and spent some time in the Fleet Prison. His son John also had a taste for looting ships, as indeed had most Cornish people in those days, but was nevertheless knighted by Queen Elizabeth. Perhaps on the principle of turning poacher into gamekeeper she made him chairman of the Commissioners for Piracy in Cornwall.

This came in very handy when his wife was charged with being involved in looting a Spanish ship in the harbour and murdering the crew. She was tried by the Commissioners, with Sir John in the chair. Her Ladyship was acquitted; her fellow defendants were all hanged.

With parents like that, small wonder that John Killigrew the Third was rather a mixed-up kid. He became a gambler and general ne'er-do-well, and ended his days in jail. But John the Fourth was a much steadier chap; he built the first lighthouse at the Lizard and got another knighthood. Unfortunately his wife took after the earlier Killigrews. She plundered a Dutch vessel and had an affair with an officer of the Pendennis garrison. John spent what was left of his inheritance on divorce proceedings.

His brother Sir Peter succeeded him and things began to look up. He obtained Falmouth's town charter, his son built the Town Quay, now the Customs House Quay, and the Killigrew fortunes were restored. But the second Peter left only a daughter, and although her husband Martin Lister took the name of Killigrew they died childless. Martin Lister Killigrew had the memorial erected in 1737 as 'a beautiful embellishment to the town'. He instructed his steward it should have no details on the inscription – 'not so much as the date of the year' – but it is said that details of the family history were put in a bottle and sealed in the memorial, thus depriving the public of a first-class read. It is also said that, not to be outdone, the workmen on the memorial put their names in another bottle and sealed that in too. The memorial has been moved twice since, but the bottles have kept their secrets.

There is nothing secret about the Ashton Memorial at **Lancaster**, which dominates the town. When Lord Ashton erected it in 1906 in memory of his wife he was obviously determined that all its features should be displayed as ostentatiously as possible. The only slight mystery about it is the steam locomotive which is carved upon it, since Lord

The Killigrew Memorial at Falmouth is a discreet reminder of a remarkable family (left). The Ashton Memorial at Lancaster is anything but discreet; it dominates the town (below).

Southampton's memorials range from Sir Bevis (above) who in spite of his fancy skirt slew a giant and was so tall he could walk through the Solent, to the Gas Column in honour of a local MP who presented the columns for the town's gaslights – he also happened to be chairman of the gas company (right).

Ashton made his fortune not from trains but from lino. However, if the Lord of the Manor decides to spend £87,000 – even at today's prices – on a memorial which looks like a junior version of St Paul's Cathedral, not many people are going to argue about the odd steam engine – particularly as he paid for a new Town Hall as well.

Southampton has a remarkable assortment of memorials, from the genuinely monumental Sir Bevis on Bar Gate, an heroic character in spite of his fancy skirt, who slew a giant and was tall enough to walk through the Solent, to the more contemporary Gas Column on a traffic island in Queen's Way. The Gas Column is in honour of a Southampton MP, William Chamberlayne, not as a tribute to his loquaciousness but to thank him for 'his munificent gift of the iron columns supporting the public lights of the town'.

The gift was not as munificent as all that, since Mr Chamberlayne was chairman of the gas company, and his gaslights would have looked a bit silly if there had been no columns to put them on. But he had earlier erected an obelisk in Mayfield Park in honour of a fellow politician, Charles James Fox, so perhaps it was only fair he should get one himself.

Edward Simeon of **Reading** was not a member of the Obelisk Old Boys' Network, and had to pay for his own. It stands in Reading Market Place, ostensibly as 'a mark of affection to his native town', though it is difficult to see what use his native town could put it to. As it has turned out, the lower section has

Edward Simeon erected his memorial in Reading 'as a mark of affection to his native town'. His native town obscured it with public conveniences (far left). The Percy Tenantry Column was erected at Alnwick by the tenants in gratitude for having their rents reduced (left and below). The Percys considered this an expensive extravagance and put up their rents again. It was enough to make the lion's tail stand on end . . .

been largely obscured by pillbox-like public conveniences. The monument consists of a triangular pillar with a torch on top; this might have been very handy if the torch could be lit, but like the rest of the pillar it is made of Portland stone.

Another obelisk which did not have quite the effect that was planned is at the southern entrance to **Alnwick** in Northumberland, the Percy Tenantry Column. It stands 83 feet high, an elegant fluted column with a lion on top, emblem of the Percys, who have been Dukes of Northumberland for centuries. It was a gesture of gratitude from the tenants when their rents were reduced – but the gesture backfired. The duke was so astonished to find they could afford such an expensive tribute that he promptly put up their rents again. This of course was before the days of trades unions and tenants' associations; the same mistake by the tenants, or by the duke, is not likely to happen again.

Monuments on unusual sites. The Crimean War Memorial at Sheffield was chopped into sections and became a kind of adventure playground (above); only the base and the statue remain (right). Castle Cary has its war memorial in a pond (below), a useful defence against vandals, but laying wreaths could be a problem.

The most common form of monument must be the war memorial, to be found in virtually every town in the land, commemorating the fallen of two World Wars, and occasionally of wars before that. **Sheffield**, for instance, has a Crimean War Memorial, which used to stand at the Moorhead, but after a century fell – almost literally – on hard times. When it was moved to the Botanical Gardens in 1960 the lofty stone pillar was chopped up into sections and taken away to be used as a sort of adventure playground, while the statue of Victory which once perched level with the house-tops now sits humbly on the base.

Castle Cary in Somerset had a more interesting idea for its war memorial – it put it in the middle of a pond. This effectively protects it from vandals, but does it present problems for laying wreaths on Remembrance Day? Do they drain the pond, or lay a plank across, or just wear thigh-boots? If you want the answer, be in Castle Cary next Remembrance Sunday. However they manage it, this must be one of the most attractively sited memorials in the country, thanks to a local solicitor called R. B. Drewitt, who presented the pond to the town for this purpose. The pond itself has quite a history; it is said to be part of the old castle moat, and in the days of summary local justice was used for ducking scolds and witches.

Occasionally one finds a memorial to that special brand of war hero, a pilot who lost his life through flying his damaged plane away from a populated area, to crash in open country. There is

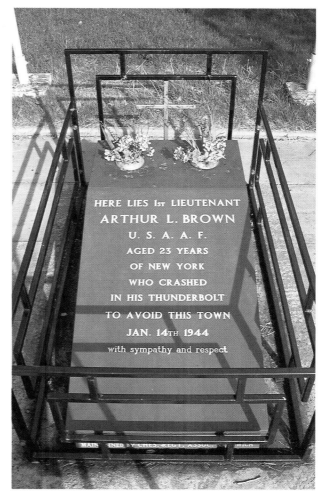

HERE LIES 1st LIEUTENANT
ARTHUR L. BROWN
U. S. A. A. F.
AGED 23 YEARS
OF NEW YORK
WHO CRASHED
IN HIS THUNDERBOLT
TO AVOID THIS TOWN
JAN. 14TH 1944
with sympathy and respect

one at **Wallingford** in Oxfordshire to commemorate two Canadian fliers, Flying Officer J. A. Wilding and Sgt. J. F. Andrew, who in 1944 remained at the controls of their crippled bomber, which was carrying a full bomb-load, and flew it clear of the town to crash and explode in open fields.

Their supreme sacrifice and conspicuous gallantry almost certainly saved the lives of many of the town's inhabitants

says the inscription. The memorial stands at the junction of Wilding Road and Andrew Road, named in their honour.

A similar story lies behind the name of Brown Road in **Nantwich**, Cheshire. Also in 1944, 23-year-old Lieut. Arthur L.

Brown of the United States Air Force stayed at the controls of his disabled Thunderbolt fighter in order to avoid the town centre. His grave on the bank of the river just outside the town marks the spot where he crashed.

In 1988 **Norwich** City Council were urged to erect a similar plaque on Mousehold Heath, on the edge of the city, to commemorate the crews of two wartime bombers who, they were told, 'with their own deaths only seconds away, were selfless enough to consider the safety of those below them, and make deliberate changes of course in order to crash on open heath instead of the built-up area around it'. If no plaque has yet materialised, perhaps this mention of them will serve as a reminder of their courage.

Gallant airmen commemorated at Wallingford (above, left) and Nantwich (above) for sacrificing their own chances of survival in order to prevent their aircraft from crashing on the town.

Memorials to men who risked or lost their lives, in a train explosion (left), in the plague (above) or at sea (below).

This kind of sacrifice is not confined to pilots. **Soham** in Cambridgeshire has a plaque to the memory of engine driver Ben Gimbert and his fireman, James Nightall, who were taking an ammunition train through the town when one waggon caught fire. They uncoupled it from the rest of the train and attempted to haul it into open country, but after 100 yards it blew up, killing James Nightall and a signalman who was nearby. Ben Gimbert was severely injured but survived. Much damage was done, but their action probably saved the town from complete devastation.

Salisbury has a memorial for a much earlier display of gallantry, of quite a different kind. When the city was hit by plague in 1627 most of the citizens fled, but the Mayor, John Ivie, stayed at his duties and fought the outbreak almost single-handed except for two constables, whose names are also on the plaque. In this case it was not just 40 years but three centuries before the authorities recognised their devotion.

Natural perils on land and at sea have given rise to many memorials for those who perished by them. The monument on **Liverpool** Pier was originally in memory of the engine-room staff of the ill-fated *Titanic*, but it now commemorates all such engineers who have been lost at sea. Other members of the *Titanic*'s crew are remembered at Southampton, while at **Falmouth** there is a memorial to the men of the Post Office Packet Service, who were based in the town and faced similar hazards delivering the mail all over the world between 1688 and 1852.

On land, mining has caused many disasters and many deaths. **Barnsley**, in the heart of the South Yorkshire coalfield, has one of the most dramatic of these memorials on Kendray Hill, marking the deaths of over 350 men and boys during a series of explosions in the Old Oaks colliery in 1866. It records in particular the bravery of two men who went down the pit to rescue the sole survivor.

It is a long time since Britain was invaded, but there are still reminders around of when it happened. The earliest is recalled by a plaque near **Deal** Castle in Kent, which claims that this was where Julius Caesar landed in 55 BC. Actually the coastline in those parts has changed considerably in the last 2000 years, so perhaps it should not be taken too literally.

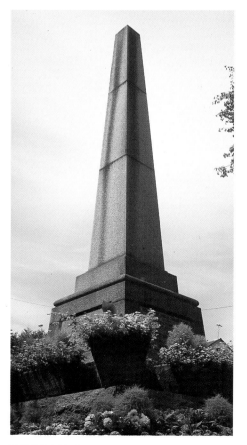

Two monuments in memory of men who died underground and at sea. At Barnsley they remember the men and boys who died during a series of explosions in the Old Oaks Colliery, and the two men who rescued the sole survivor (above and left). At Falmouth they remember the men of the Post Office Packet Service who sailed with the mail from this harbour to all parts of the world (far left).

Memories of sea battles and the risk of invasion. A column at Swanage recalls how King Alfred fought off the Danes – the cannon-balls on top of it were invented a little later (right). The guns at Southwold (below) were provided by George II after the town complained it was 'naked and exposed to the insults of the Common Enemys'. Happily they were never needed.

A column at **Swanage** records that this was where King Alfred fought off the Danish fleet in a great naval battle in AD 877. Rather anachronistically the column is topped with cannon-balls, which Alfred would no doubt have been grateful for, but they hadn't been invented at the time. Maybe he bombarded the Danes with those burnt cakes instead. The cannon-balls were actually captured in the Crimea, nearly 1800 years later; presumably the city fathers couldn't think where else to put them.

While Swanage remembers fending off the Danes and Plymouth remembers how the Spaniards never made it, in Suffolk they recall being menaced by the French. The good burghers of **Southwold** complained to George II that 'this place is in a very dangerous condition for want of guns and ammunition, being naked and exposed to the insults of the Common Enemys'. George II, duly impressed, gave them some ageing eighteen-pounders, which happily never had to be fired in anger. They were put in store during the last war – not even the Home Guard could find a use for them – and they are now back in place overlooking the sea front.

A French invasion force did actually land in Britain in 1797, but not in the manner they intended. They were aiming to capture Bristol, but a gale blew them off course and they finished up near **Fishguard**. Twelve hundred of them came ashore with only the vaguest idea where they were, and one delightful story has it that they encountered a group of Welshwomen wearing their traditional red cloaks, mistook them for guardsmen, and surrendered forthwith. It wasn't really quite as simple as that; they were actually captured by local troops commanded by Baron Cawdor, Fishguard's eighteenth-century equivalent to Captain Mainwaring. I gather the Frenchmen were mostly conscripted convicts who didn't want to be there in the first place, but full marks to Baron Cawdor anyway. An inscribed stone tells the story.

A very different reminder of another unplanned French landing is to be found at **Hartlepool**. During the Napoleonic wars a French ship was wrecked offshore, and only one survivor reached land – the ship's monkey. This unfortunate creature was promptly hanged by the sturdy folk of Hartlepool – because, so local legend says, it would not respond to interrogation, so they assumed it must be a French spy. Curiously this macabre little incident is commemorated by the town's rugby football club, which has the emblem of a hanging monkey on its club tie. Any visiting team intending to take a mascot with them to Hartlepool, or even the family pet, should ensure it can talk . . .

The last invasion of England from north of the border, apart from football supporters, was in 1745, and the defeat of the Jacobite uprising at Culloden is marked by a lofty octagonal tower – not at Culloden but a lot further south at **Richmond** in Yorkshire. The connection is not immediately obvious, but it seems that the local landowner who erected it, a Mr Yorke, had a son who fought in the battle. He wanted to celebrate not only his son's survival, but 'the crushing finally and forever of any hopes for the return to the throne of Britain of the house of Stewart'. Mr Yorke's loathing of the Stuarts was so strong it even affected his

spelling. The tower was built a year or so after the battle, complete with some very fancy Gothic trimmings, and it still stands on a hill just outside the town, functioning these days as a high-rise holiday cottage.

More invasion memories. A French force landed by mistake at Fishguard; one story says they saw Welshwomen in red shawls, mistook them for guardsmen and surrendered. The plaque tells the real facts.

The tower outside Richmond (left) was built to celebrate driving back the Scots at Culloden. The hanged monkey of Hartlepool (below) is a reminder of how a more pathetic 'invasion' was dealt with.

A piece of piping in Shanklin Chine is a reminder of PLUTO, the pipeline under the ocean which carried fuel to the Normandy beaches after D-Day (above).

More ancient relics by the roadside: the London Stone at Staines marking the boundary of the City's jurisdiction (below) and the Bail boundary stone in Lincoln (right) marking the outer bailey round the castle.

Lastly on invasions, a reminder of one which actually succeeded – but in this case it was the British who were doing the invading. In the very peaceful surroundings of **Shanklin Chine** on the Isle of Wight there is a section of PLUTO, the pipeline under the ocean, which was laid across the Channel to carry fuel to the invading forces on the Normandy beaches in 1944. It was the earliest Channel tunnel – but only a foot or so wide.

Another group of monuments marks ancient boundaries and notable journeys. The City of London may be popularly known as the Square Mile but its jurisdiction extended much further than that. Its western limit was marked by the London Stone near the parish church at **Staines**, which even with today's urban spread is hardly regarded as part of the metropolis. A new pedestal has been provided but the original stone stands on it, inscribed

God Preserve the City of London
AD1285.

Lincoln has preserved a boundary stone which shows how far the jurisdiction of the Bail extended. This had nothing to do with remand courts or cricket; the Bail took its name from the outer bailey of the castle, which enclosed the upper city. The boundary is marked by a modest little pillar set in the footpath, easy to mistake for the sort which water boards and telephone companies like to plant on the roadside, but of considerable historical interest none the less.

Oswestry has a stone which marks the point of safety outside the old town walls where the markets were held during time of plague in the sixteenth century. It is called the Croeswylan Stone, the Cross of Weeping, and there is a hollow in it which might have taken the shaft of a cross. Alternatively the hollow might have been used as a bowl in which to wash money suspected of contamination. Then again it could just be a stone with a hole in it.

Of the monuments erected to mark journeys, perhaps the best known are the Eleanor Crosses which Edward I left behind at each stopping place of his wife's funeral cortege as it travelled from

Nottinghamshire to Westminster Abbey. The remains of the first one are in the castle gateway at **Lincoln** – it was here that her body was embalmed. Another survives at **Northampton** on the London Road, and the Geddington Cross at **Kettering** has been incorporated in the borough's coat of arms. But a much lesser known pilgrimage is marked by an obelisk at the end of **Marlow** High Street in Buckinghamshire. Even today the sight of it must make members of the Cecil family wince. The Cecils of Hatfield House used to suffer considerably from gout, and travelled regularly to Bath to take the waters. The memorial marks one of the stopping places on what became known as the Gout Track.

The Sack Stone – or, just as accurately, the Stone Sack – is said to mark a stopping place on a very different journey. It is on Fonaby Top, just outside **Caistor** in Lincolnshire, and legend has it that Jesus was riding through the fields – in Lincolnshire? – when he saw men sowing corn and asked for some to feed His donkey. The inhospitable farmer said he had no corn to give, and when Jesus pointed to the grain sack he claimed it was merely a sack-shaped stone. 'Stone be it!' said Jesus, and stone it became. Various powers have been attributed to it ever since, but none to equal the power of local imagination . . .

There is no doubt, however, about the authenticity of the three journeys which

The Cross of Weeping at Oswestry (below) – is the hole to take a cross, or to wash contaminated money, or just another hole?

The memorial at Marlow which marks a stopping place on the route to Bath to take the water and cure the gout (left) – known of course as the Gout Track.

'Stone be it!' Was the Sack Stone at Caistor (left) created by a miracle?

are commemorated at **Dover**, though at the time they too might have been considered beyond the power of men. Two of the memorials are on the East Cliff promenade, to Captain West who was the first man to swim the Channel, and to C. S. Rolls, the first to fly the Channel both ways. But the most unusual of the three memorials, a granite silhouette of a monoplane set in the ground, is to the man who flew the Channel first, a year ahead of Rolls. It has not been given such a prominent position; M. Bleriot after all was a Frenchman.

Finally a monument which commemorates nothing in particular, and which I only include because the sculptor gives quite the most disarming reason for putting it there. It stands at the entrance to the Royal Priors in **Leamington Spa**, and it was considered of such moment that the Queen agreed to unveil it in 1988. Its title is 'Elephants and Boy', and that is precisely what it is – three bronze elephants with a boy sitting on one of them. But why elephants in Leamington Spa?

The local press put the question to the sculptor, Nicholas Dimbleby – yes, one of *those* Dimblebys. He talked rather grandly at first about the town's colonial connections, and how its growth had been linked with the growth of the Empire.

Then he got to the real point.

'Anyway,' he said, 'I like elephants.'

All right, said the local press, but why put them in Leamington Spa?

'Because', he said simply, 'I thought Leamington was the kind of place where elephants would be happy.'

It is that kind of reasoning which makes it possible to write this kind of book . . .

The monoplane silhouette at Dover, a very appropriate memorial to M. Bleriot's first flight across the Channel (below). But is the little boy on the elephant appropriate for Leamington Spa? (right) 'Certainly', said the sculptor; 'Leamington is the kind of place where an elephant would be happy!' There is nothing to follow that . . .

MAPS

The maps on the following pages are intended for general reference only. They are not recommended as route maps. The use of your regular route planner is therefore advisable.

MAP 1

Cleveland
Cumbria
Durham
Tyne & Wear

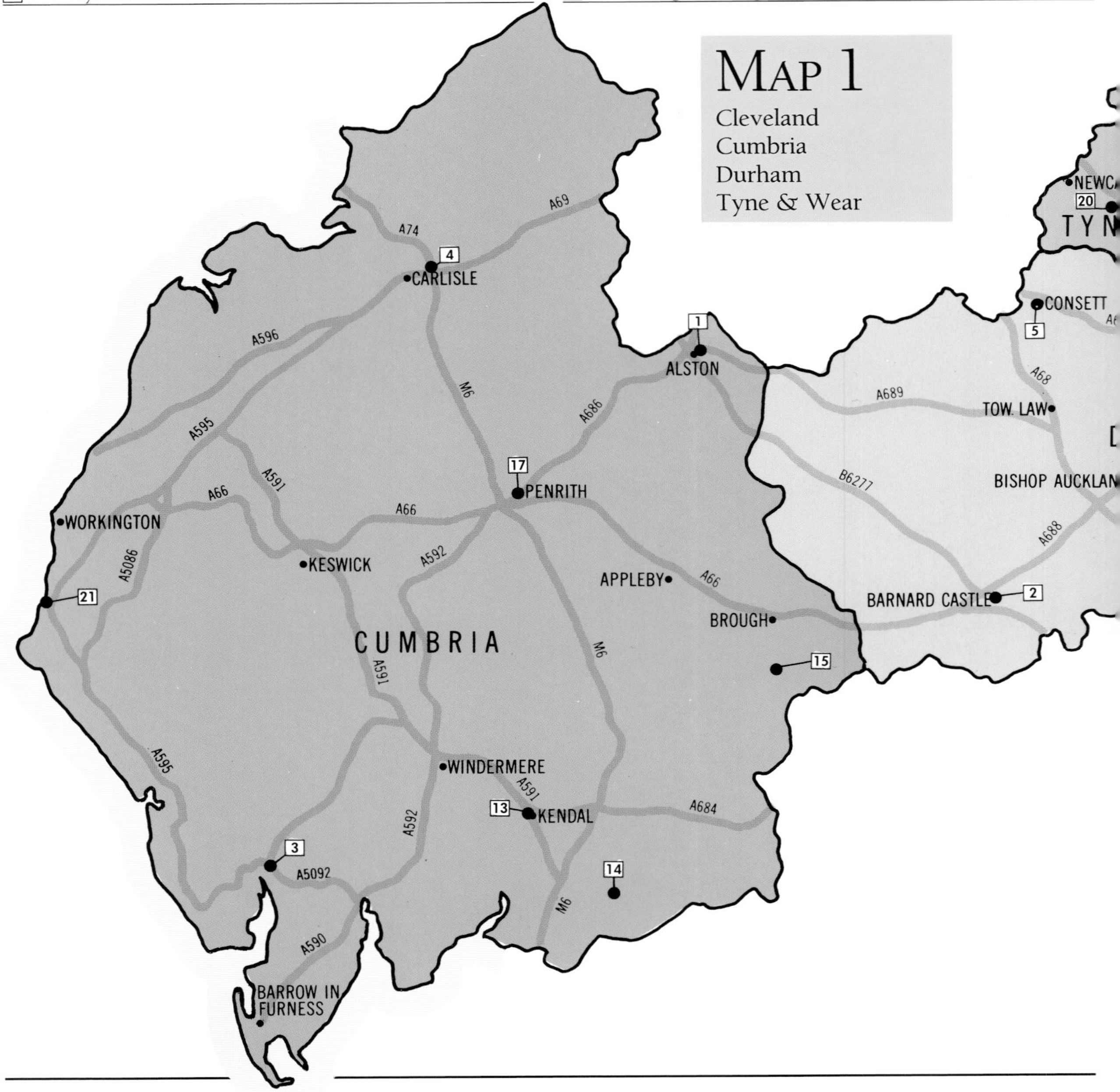

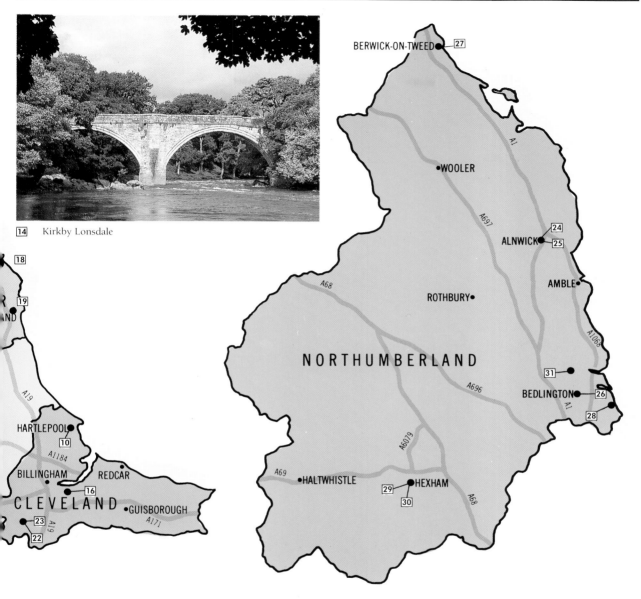

14 Kirkby Lonsdale

BERWICK-ON-TWEED 27

•WOOLER

A1

A697

ALNWICK 24
25

A68

AMBLE

ROTHBURY•

A1068

NORTHUMBERLAND

A696

31
BEDLINGTON 26
A1
28

A6079

A69

•HALTWHISTLE 29 •HEXHAM
30

A68

18

19
R
AND

A19

HARTLEPOOL
10

A1184

BILLINGHAM •REDCAR

CLEVELAND •GUISBOROUGH

A171
A19

23
22

MAP 2
Northumberland

MAP 3

Humberside
North Yorkshire
South Yorkshire
West Yorkshire

| 68 | York |

STOKESLEY

RICHMOND 53
54
55

NORTHALLERTON

HAWES

THIRSK

NORTH YORKSHIRE

SETTLE 59

48
49

HARROGATE

YORK 68
69

ILKLEY

32

36
37

LEEDS

BRADFORD 44
39

WEST YORKSHIRE

SELBY

45

MORLEY

41
42
43

WAKEFIELD 67

52

HUDDERSFIELD

46

THORNE

BARNSLEY

33

DONCASTER

SOUTH YORKSHIRE

ROTHERHAM 56

66 60
SHEFFIELD 61
65 62
64 63

32   Aberford

MAP 4

Cheshire
Greater Manchester
Isle of Man
Lancashire
Merseyside

MAP 5

Derbyshire
Lincolnshire
Nottinghamshire

MAP 6

Hereford
   & Worcester
Leicester
Shropshire
Staffordshire
Warwickshire
West Midlands

170 Stoke-on-Trent

A53

A523

TRENT

A50

A518 174

SHIRE

RD BURTON UPON TRENT•

A51 A515 A38

136 152

A5
LICHFIELD
153 A453

ALL 175

M6

•SUTTON COLDFIELD

•WEST BROMWICH
132
RMINGHAM 133
131 134

WEST MIDLANDS

SOLIHULL A45

M42 A43

160
DDITCH

A34 A41 178
177 176 WARWICK

WARWICKSHIRE

A422

171

A439 STRATFORD UPON AVON

172 A46 A41

ESHAM 140
141

A34

NUNEATON•

M6

•BEDWORTH

137
139
138 COVENTRY•
A45 RUGBY•

KENILWORTH• 147
148

167

A453

A607

SHEPSHED• •LOUGHBOROUGH •MELTON MOWBRAY

COALVILLE• A50
A6 A606

LEICESTERSHIRE OAKHAM•

149 A47
150 •LEICESTER
UPPINGHAM•

M1 A6

•HINCKLEY

A5

MARKET HARBOROUGH• 155

131 Birmingham

MAP 7

Avon
Berkshire
Buckinghamshire
Gloucestershire
Hampshire
Isle of Wight
Oxfordshire
Wiltshire

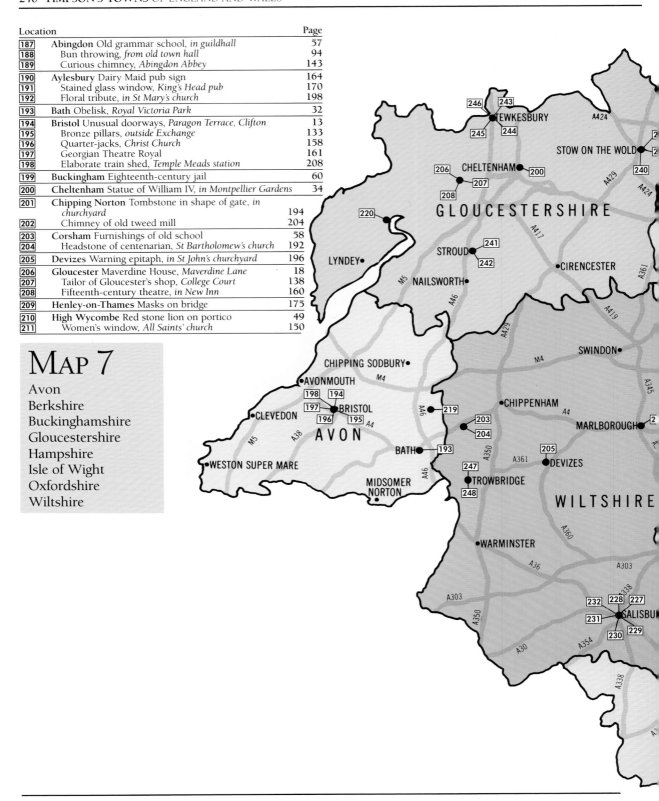

MAP 8

Bedfordshire
Cambridgeshire
Essex
Hertfordshire
Northamptonshire

280 Harlow

WISBECH 306
A47
ERBOROUGH
MARCH
A10
RAMSEY
A142
A141
ELY 276
277
278
CAMBRIDGESHIRE 302
301
303
A604
EOTS 267
CAMBRIDGE 268
269
270
A14
M11
A11

ROYSTON
261
BALDOCK
298
SAFFRON WALDEN
299
A131
STEVENAGE
A120
HALSTEAD
A604
273
COLCHESTER 274
279
266
272
A12
BRAINTREE
A120
A12
A120
281
282
TFORDSHIRE
A131
A133
CLACTON-ON-SEA
A10
305 WARE
ESSEX
283
280 M11
S
293
294
POTTERS BAR
CHELMSFORD 271
EPPING
A12
ENFIELD
M11
M25
A130
M1
A10
A127
ROMFORD
BASILDON
HAMPSTEAD
DAGENHAM
A13
SOUTHEND ON SEA
A13
ATER LONDON
FORD
A2
304
M20
WIMBLEDON
SIDCUP
CROYDON
M23

293   Maldon

MAP 9

East Sussex
Kent
Surrey
West Sussex

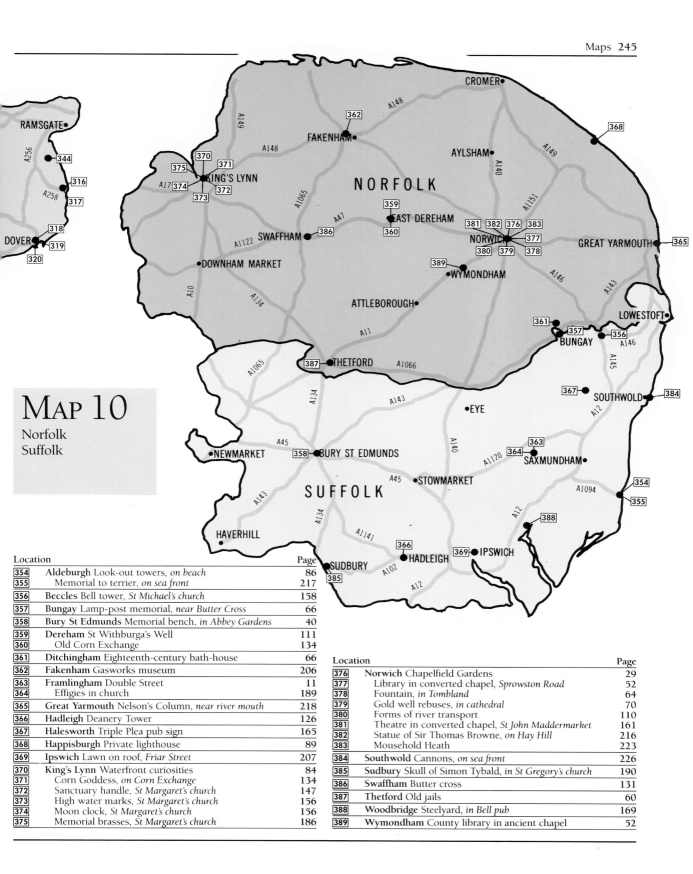

MAP 10

Norfolk
Suffolk

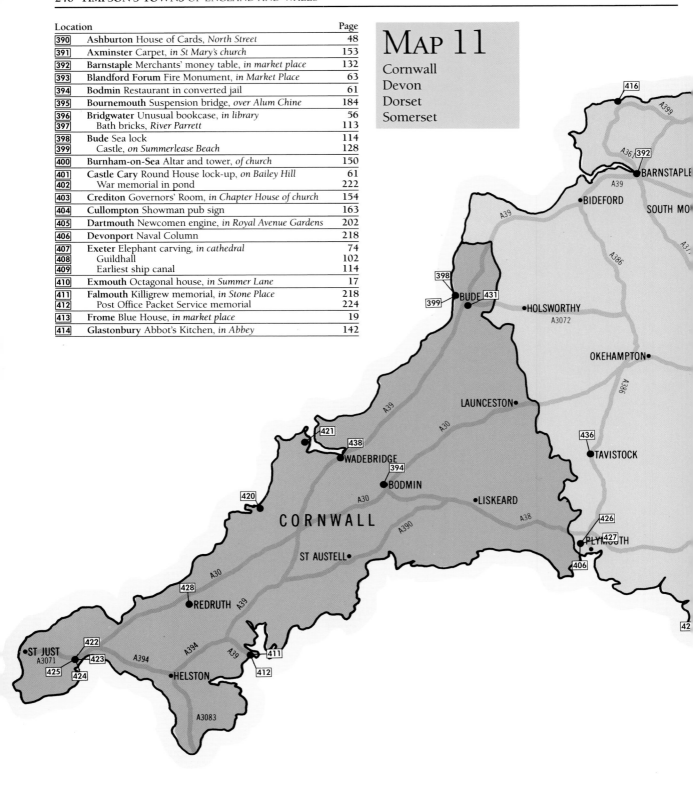

MAP 11

Cornwall
Devon
Dorset
Somerset

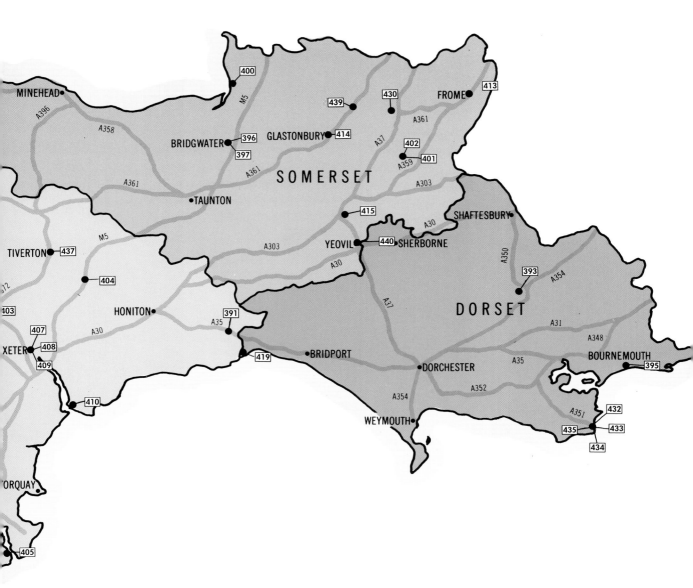

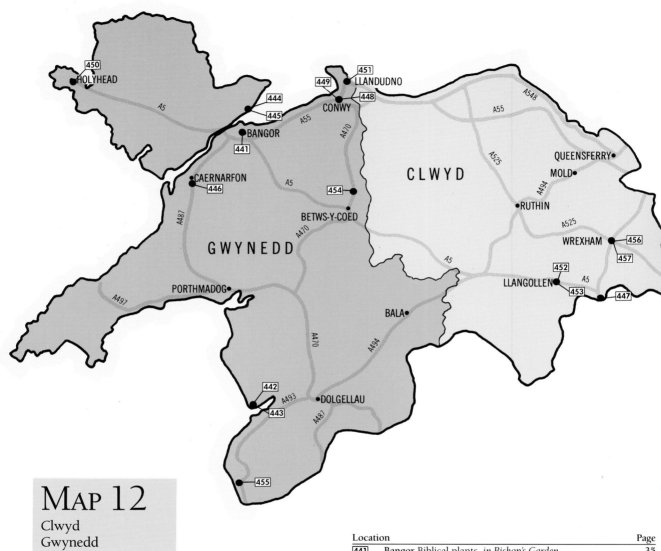

MAP 12
Clwyd
Gwynedd

MAP 13
Powys

451   Llandudno

MAP 14

Dyfed
Gwent
Mid Glamorgan
South Glamorgan
West Glamorgan

477 Pembroke

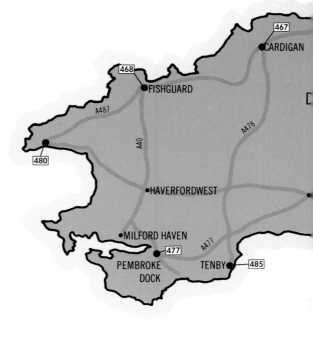

A487

A485

●ABERYSTWYTH A44

A485

●LAMPETER

A482

A483

A485

LLANDOVERY● 470

471

A40

●LLANDEILO

A483

464 Caerphilly

474

LLANELLI

WEST
GLAMORGAN A465

MERTHYR TYDFIL

A465

●ABERGAVENNY

A465

MONMOUTH 475

A40

GWENT A449

NEATH●

484 481

SWANSEA●

482

483

●PORT TALBOT

MID
GLAMORGAN

479

A470

472

M4

473

CWMBRAN●

A4042

464

469

465

CARDIFF●

466

476

M4

NEWPORT●

CHEPSTOW●

A48

478

SOUTH
GLAMORGAN

463

INDEX

INDEX
continued

ACKNOWLEDGMENTS

The majority of illustrations in this book were specially commissioned; others supplied to us or requiring acknowledgment are listed below.

17 *bottom* By kind permission of Mrs Ursula Tudor Perkins. 22 *bottom right* Kent Archaeological Rescue Unit. 23 *bottom left* By permission of Bolton Museums and Art Gallery. 24 *centre, bottom left and right* Morrison Photos; by permission of Royal Life Insurance Ltd. 36 *top* By kind permission of the Bursar, Christ's College, Cambridge. 45 By permission of the President and Fellows of Queen's College, Cambridge. 52 *top* By permission of Thomas Plume's Trustees. 52 *bottom left and right* By kind permission of W. B. Gledhill, Clerk to the Wymondham Old Grammar School Foundation. 53 *top* By permission of Norwich City Council. 53 *bottom right* By kind permission of the Richmondshire Museum. 56 *bottom left and right* By permission of the Warden and Scholars of Winchester College. 59 *bottom left* By permission of the Lawrence Cloisters Trust Ltd. 63 *top* By permission of Anglian Water. 71 By permission of the Provost of Southwell Minster. 72 *bottom left and right* By permission of the Provost and Canons of Blackburn Cathedral. 74 *top left and right* By permission of the Dean and Chapter of Hereford Cathedral. 75 *top left and right* By permission of the Dean and Chapter of Salisbury Cathedral. 75 *bottom* By kind permission of the Dean and Chapter of York. 76 By permission of the Dean and Chapter of Chester Cathedral. 77 The Dean and Chapter Library, Durham Cathedral. 78 By permission of the Dean and Chapter of Guildford Cathedral. 79 By permission of the Dean and Chapter of Ely Cathedral. 82 By permission of the Dean and Chapter of Peterborough Cathedral. 84 *top and centre* By permission of King's Lynn Preservation Trust Limited. 84 *bottom* By permission of Norfolk County Council. 85 By kind permission of Mr W. Foster. 101 By permission of Warwickshire County Council. 102 *top* By permission of North Bedfordshire Borough Council. 106 Reproduced by permission of Glynn Vivian Art Gallery, Swansea, and Mr Rodney Brangwyn. 110 By permission of Norfolk Museums Service. 120 By kind permission of Major I. B. Ramsden. 121 By kind permission of the Earl of Powys. 122 *top* Reproduced by permission of the Dean and Canons of Windsor. 123 *bottom left and right* By permission of the National Trust. 137 *top left* Reproduced by permission of Mr A. Guy. 140 *top* Reproduced by kind permission of the Co-operative Union, Manchester. 143 *Bottom two* By permission of the Friends of Abingdon. 148 *top* By kind permission of Tilehouse Baptist Church. 149 Hans Raj; by permission of the Vicar and Church Wardens, St John's Church. 160 *centre* By kind permission of Mr J. Meier. 161 *bottom* By permission of the Trust of the Maddermarket Theatre. 184 *top* By permission of Tyne and Wear Passenger Transport Authority. 189 By kind permission of Canon Pitcher. 190 *top left and right* By permission of the Rector and Church Wardens, St Gregory's parish church. 190 *bottom right* By permission of the Master and Fellows of Sidney Sussex College, Cambridge. 210 *bottom left* By permission of the Buttermarket, Howard Street. 228 *top* Thearle Photography; by kind permission of Mrs Anne Springman.

The maps appearing on pages 231 to 251 are based upon the Ordnance Survey map with the permission of the Controller of HMSO, Crown copyright reserved.

Every effort has been made to obtain the appropriate rights or permission to publish all copyright material. The publishers would be pleased to acknowledge any omission in future editions.

The publishers wish to express their gratitude to the many individuals and organisations whose specialised knowledge was invaluable in the preparation of this book. Also to Helen Thompson for her tireless efforts in the coordination of this publication.